MASTER THE
STRATEGIES

EFFECTIVE TECHNIQUES AND METHODS TO IMPROVE YOUR TOEIC TEST SCORE

STUDENT WORKBOOK

CHRIS QUINN

ARKADIAN INTERMEDIA ENTERPRISES LLC   *MASTER ENGLISH SERIES*

Quinn, Chris, 1970-
Master the TOEIC Strategies Student Workbook: Effective Techniques and Methods to improve your TOEIC test score / by Chris Quinn.

ISBN-10: 0-9849268-0-1
ISBN-13: 978-0-9849268-0-0

Published by Arkadian InterMedia Enterprises LLC
www.masterthetoeic.com

A quick word from Chris

I hope this book, *Master the TOEIC: Strategies Student Workbook*, has been helpful. It is my goal to make sure you get the TOEIC score you want. If there is anything in this book that you don't understand, please contact me. I can't tell you how many countless hours are spent putting together the information into this book. If you know someone who would like to receive Master the TOEIC: Strategies, please have them come to www.masterthetoeic.com to purchase a copy. Each purchase goes toward inspiring me to create more and better Master English books in the future. Thank you.

Warm regards,

Chris Quinn
President & Founder
Arkadian InterMedia Enterprises LLC
chris@masterthetoeic.com

TABLE OF CONTENTS

The three most important strategies in this book:

"Become a TOEIC Sherlock Holmes"

"Focus on what is <u>wrong</u>, not what is <u>right</u>"

"<u>Actively</u> listen and read TOEIC-like English every day"

Study EVERY question and transcript for words or grammar you don't understand.

The Structure of the TOEIC Test

Listening Section

100 questions = 45 minutes

1: **Photographs**	10 Questions		
2: **Question-Response**	30 Questions		
3: **Conversations**	30 Questions	10 Conversations	*(3 Questions each)*
4: **Short Talks**	30 Questions	10 Talks	*(3 Questions each)*

- You will have about 8 seconds to answer each question.

- You SHOULD NOT turn the page in the test booklet to see the next page or section until you are told to do so.

- You MUST wait till the Test Narrator tells you to turn the page.

- You SHOULD NOT write in the Test Booklet, but some test centers do not enforce this.

Reading Section

100 questions = 75 minutes

5: **Incomplete Sentences**	40 Questions		
6: **Text Completion**	12 Questions	3 texts	*(4 Questions each)*
		or 4 texts	*(3 Questions each)*
7: **Reading Comprehension**	28 Questions	7-10 single texts	*(2-5 Questions each)*
	20 Questions	4 double texts	*(5 Questions each)*

- You can answer Questions from any Part in any order.

- Do the easiest parts of the Reading Section first; do the hardest part last.

- You SHOULD NOT write in the Test Booklet, but some test centers do not enforce this.

> You need to effectively pace yourself in the Reading Section—don't spend too much time in any one Section or Question.

Recommended Study Schedule - *Month 1*

Sunday	Monday	Tuesday	Wednesday	Thursday	Friday	Saturday
Strategy Exercises: **Photographs**	*Open Book Practice:* **Photograph** *(Untimed)*	*Strategy Exercises:* **Incomplete Sentences**	*Open Book Practice:* **Incomplete Sentences** *(Untimed)*	*Study Grammar & Vocab*	*Quiz & Review:* **Photographs & Incomplete Sentences** *(Timed)*	*Study Grammar & Vocab*
Strategy Exercises: **Question-Response**	*Open Book Practice:* **Question-Response** *(Untimed)*	*Strategy Exercises:* **Text Completion**	*Open Book Practice:* **Text Completion** *(Untimed)*	*Study Grammar & Vocab*	*Quiz & Review:* **Question-Response & Text Completion** *(Timed)*	*Study Grammar & Vocab*
Strategy Exercises: **Short Conversations**	*Open Book Practice:* **Short Conversations** *(Untimed)*	*Strategy Exercises:* **Reading Comprehension**	*Open Book Practice:* **Reading Comprehension** *(Untimed)*	*Study Grammar & Vocab*	*Quiz & Review:* **Short Conversations & Reading Comprehension** *(Timed)*	*Study Grammar & Vocab*
Strategy Exercises: **Short Talks**	*Open Book Practice:* **Short Talks** *(Untimed)*	*Strategy Exercises:* **Reading Comprehension**	*Open Book Practice:* **Reading Comprehension** *(Untimed)*	*Study Grammar & Vocab*	*Quiz & Review:* **Short Talks & Reading Comprehension** *(Timed)*	*Study Grammar & Vocab*

Months 2 & 3

Sunday	Monday	Tuesday	Wednesday	Thursday	Friday	Saturday
Full TOEIC Practice Test	**Review TOEIC Practice Test**	*Break*	*Study Grammar & Vocab*	*Study Grammar & Vocab*	*Study Grammar & Vocab*	*Break*

Explanation of recommended Study Schedule

"Strategy Exercises"   Read the chapter from *Master the TOEIC: Strategies* for a specific Part. Study its Method, Strategies, and Tricks. Do the Exercises in *Master the TOEIC: Strategies* for that part of the TOEIC.

"Open Book Practice"   Using your own Practice Test book, do one or two complete quizzes for that specific part of the TOEIC (Example: if you studied the strategies for Part 2: Question-Response the day before, you will practice using the method by listening to one or two complete 30-question sets of Question-Responses). **THIS PRACTICE SHOULD NOT BE TIMED**. Take as much time as you need, following the Method and Strategies given in *Master the TOEIC: Strategies*—you can look at the Methods and Strategies given in this book. If you are doing Listening Questions, you can pause or replay Questions to give yourself time to find the correct answer.

"Study Grammar & Vocab"   Focus on grammar issues you did not understand in Incomplete Sentences & Text Completion parts of the TOEIC. Also, look at all Transcripts, Questions, Answer Choices and Texts for vocabulary words you do know yet know.

"Quiz & Review"   Using your own Practice Test book, do a complete Quiz for two Parts of the TOEIC. **THIS QUIZ SHOULD BE TIMED**. See the **TOEIC Practice Test Answer Grid** (*Page 8*) for a list of the amount of time we recommend you use for each Reading Section. After you finish your quizzes, you will want to check your answers. For EVERY QUESTION YOU GOT WRONG, try and figure out what **Trick** they used and why you got it wrong.

After you have studied every chapter of Master the TOEIC: Strategies, and practiced using the Method, begin to practice taking complete TOEIC Tests (all 7 parts!). Review each test the day after you took it. Focus on wrong answers and what Tricks they used.

Do NOT study for the TOEIC more than 4 hours each day.

After you have studied Methods and Strategies in this book, take a full TOEIC Test 1 or 2 times a week until Test Day.

You will need about 2-3 months of practice to *Master the TOEIC* using the strategies and methods in this book.

TOEIC Practice Test Answer Grid

Photocopy this page and use it when taking Quizzes and Practice Tests.

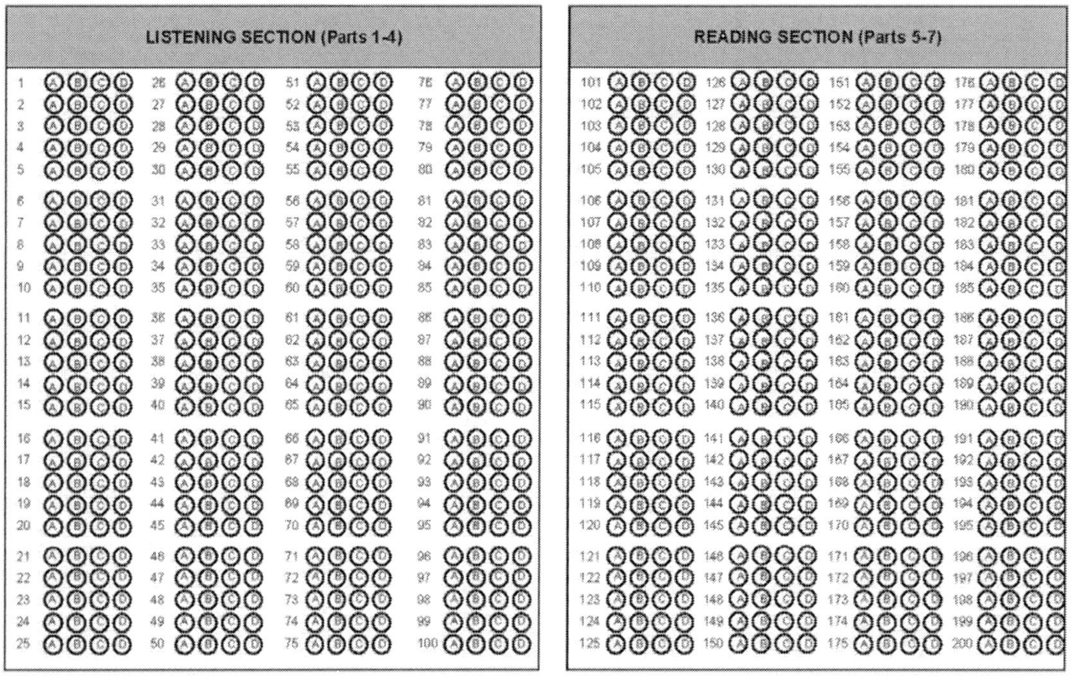
LISTENING SECTION (Parts 1-4)
READING SECTION (Parts 5-7)

Test Part	Date	# Correct	# Incorrect	% of Total	Time
Part 1					***~6 min***
Part 2					***~11 min***
Part 3					***~11 min***
Part 4					***~16 min***
Part 5					***15 min***
Part 6					***10 min***
Part 7					***50 min***

No choice for time or speed (Parts 1–4)

Choosing Key Words

What are Key Words? Why are they important in the TOEIC?

The **best Key Words** are:

- Unique to the Question or Answer Choice

- A strong Adjective

- A strong Action Verb

- A word with few or no synonyms

What are good Key Words in these Question and Answer Choices?

What words are not good Key Words?

1. Who needs to inform Mall security?

    (A) Security guards at Weston Mall
    (B) People going to dinner
    (C) Shoppers at Weston Mall
    (D) The CEO of Weston Mall

2. According to the brochure, which of the following is NOT possible?

    (A) Paying by credit card
    (B) Withdrawing on weekends
    (C) Using your ATM card overseas
    (D) Transferring money to other banks for free

3. Whom is the advertisement aimed at?

    (A) Businesses with overseas branches
    (B) Businesses in the financial sector
    (C) Real estate businesses
    (D) Computer companies

4. Which of the following ports does the ship go to?

    (A) London
    (B) Alexandria
    (C) Venice
    (D) Athens

5. What is an advantage of using Safeco?

    (A) You can withdraw money any time
    (B) You can take out Quick Loans
    (C) You can deposit money at other banks
    (D) You can write checks for free

6. What information does the caller need?

    (A) Ms. Stiles's phone number
    (B) Ms. Stiles's fax number
    (C) Ms. Stiles's social security number
    (D) Ms. Stiles's address

Scanning for Key Words

The key to Scanning is to NOT READ. You need to LOOK.

- Start by looking for the easiest Key Words first.

- Use your pencil to guide your eyes.

- Be "open" to seeing synonyms of Key Words.

- If you find a Key Word, go back and find other words from the same Question or Answer Choice.

- The farther away an Answer Choice Key Word is from Question Key Words, the less likely it is the correct answer.

- Be "open" to telling yourself "maybe" and "probably".

Which Key Words would probably be easiest to look for?

Which Key Words would probably be hardest to look for?

Which Key Words have several synonyms?

What are those synonyms?

7. What will people receive for attending the grand opening?

   (A) A coupon for a department store
   (B) A free CD from a jazz band
   (C) A tour with the city mayor
   (D) An interview on the radio

8. What is purpose of this advertisement?

   (A) To encourage calls overseas
   (B) To encourage people to change their overseas carrier
   (C) To promote an international telecommunications company
   (D) To ask how much money people spend calling overseas

9. What was NOT a result of the floods and mudslides?

   (A) Tourists canceled flights to Hawaii
   (B) Bridges were washed out
   (C) People were killed or hurt
   (D) Roads were damaged

10. Why is the woman not ready for the meeting?

   (A) The office is under reconstruction
   (B) She needs to gather more files
   (C) The photocopier does not work
   (D) She accidently deleted her report

TIP: The TOEIC often hides Key Words of correct Answer Choices by using synonyms of those Key Words.

Skimming a Text for General Information

The key to Skimming is to NOT READ. You need to ABSORB.

Focus on words that give you an understanding of the **Topic**, **Purpose**, **General Information,** or **Main Ideas.**

Focus on these types of Key Words:

- **Subject** or **Object** of each sentence

- **Action Verbs** or **Phrasal Verbs**

- **Helping Verbs**

- **Strong Adjectives**

- **Who** is doing **something** (or *requesting* something)

- **Why, when or where something is happening**

- **How** something is happening

Underline a few words for each sentence to build an understanding of the whole text

> Due to a rash of thefts at the Mall over the last month, we wish to inform you of additional security measures Weston Mall will be implementing over the next few days. To provide a more safe and secure environment for our customers, we are doubling the number of our security personnel, which will enable us to have more frequent and reliable patrolling of all areas of our complex.
>
> Security cameras are being installed at all exits. While we regret this slight intrusion of privacy, know that it is for your own protection. At the end of each week, these security tapes will be erased, to ensure that this invasion of your privacy is temporary.

Forget about READING English—begin to LOOK at English. Each word and phrase is a piece of a puzzle.

Websites to help you prepare for the TOEIC

Phrasal Verbs & Idioms

- http://www.usingenglish.com/reference/phrasal-verbs/a.html
- http://www.usingenglish.com/reference/phrasal-verbs/quizzes-verbs.html
- http://www.carolinebrownlisteninglessons.com/

English Grammar Websites

- http://www.esl.about.com *(the most complete website for explaining English)*
- http://www.better-english.com/exerciselist.html *(simpler explanations)*
- http://www.englishpage.com *(simpler explanations)*
- http://owl.english.purdue.edu/owl/resource/537/01/ *(more complex explanations)*

Business English

- http://www.masterthetoeic.com/2009/12/122209-toeic-word-list/
- http://www.learnenglishfeelgood.com/
- http://www.businessenglishsite.com/

British Accent Websites

- http://www.bbc.co.uk/worldservice/learningenglish/

English Grammar to Study

- **Verb Forms and Verb Tenses** *(especially Participles and the Verb Forms "have been" and "had been")*
- **Auxiliary Verbs** *("have to", "must", and "should" (focus on understanding what makes each of these words different from each other)*
- **Subject-Verb Agreement** *(such as "he talks" vs. "he talk")*
- **Pronouns** *(focus on when to use different forms of pronouns, such as Subjects versus Objects in sentences)*
- **Conjunctions** and **Adverb Phrases** *(focus on which conjunctions or adverbs come before Noun Clauses and which conjunctions or adverbs need Subject + Verb Clauses)*
- **Gerunds & Infinitives**
- **Prepositions**
- **Phrasal Verbs**
- **Adverb Clauses**

Other than knowing that "pound" means "dollar" and "lift" means "elevator", you don't need to know much British vocabulary.

Listen to NPR Every Day

1. Go to **www.npr.org**.

2. Click **"Programs"** on the menu bar at the top of the page.

3. Click on **"Morning Edition"** or **"All Things Considered"**.

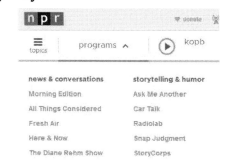

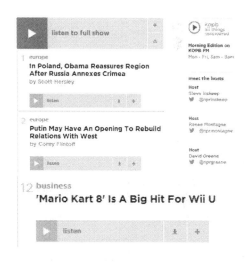

4. Scroll down page and find a news report about **Business**, **Politics**, or **Economy** that is **1 minute to 4 minutes** long.

6. Listen to the news report, taking notes on **Main Ideas**, **Major Details** and **Numbers**.

7. **Click on the news report's title** of the news report to see the transcript. Study the transcript for new words and idioms.

8. **Listen to and read the news report** at the same time for pronunciation and listening practice.

9. Close the transcript page and **listen to the news report one more time** to reinforce what you have learned.

10. Find **5 more news reports** on the same topic and listen to one each day for the next 5 days.

'Mario Kart 8' Is A Big Hit For Wii U
June 04, 2014   5:11 AM ET

The 8th edition of the classic Nintendo video game sold more than 1.2 million units its first weekend. Its new features include anti-gravity racing, allowing players to drive on walls and ceilings

Transcript

DAVID GREENE, HOST:

And our last word in Business today - go kart. Mario Kart, to be exact.

STEVE INSKEEP, HOST:

The eighth edition of the classic Nintendo video game was released on Friday and sold over 1.2 million units it's first weekend.

GREENE: Mario Kart 8 includes returning features from previous installments.

INSKEEP: The new features include antigravity racing - allowing players to drive on walls and ceilings - and Mario Kart TV, where you can upload highlights of your best races to YouTube.

GREENE: Just what I want to watch. Now despite the strong start for Mario Kart 8, the game's console, the Wii U, has been losing out to competitors.

INSKEEP: Critics say the console needs better games to attract customers. Only that would allow Wii U sales to do like those Mario Kart drivers, and defy gravity. And that's the Business News on MORNING EDITION from NPR News. I'm Steve Inskeep.

GREENE: And I'm David Greene.

Preparing for TOEIC Test Day

During the week before your TOEIC Test...

1. Wake up at the same time each day as if it *was* Test Day.

2. Visit the Test Center.

3. Practice the TOEIC at the same time of day as your Test.

4. Don't study any TOEIC the day before the Test.

5. Practice filling out the Questionnaire.
    https://docs.google.com/viewer?url=http://www.ets.org/Media/Tests/TOEIC/pdf/TOEIC_LR_examinee_handbook.pdf

Preparing for TOEIC Test Day

On the morning of your TOEIC Test...

1. Get up early enough to be at the Test Center at least 30 minutes before the test.

2. If you normally drink a lot of coffee/tea every morning, have only ONE cup.

3. On the way to the Test Center, listen to English.

4. While waiting to take the test, read English.

Reducing Stress During the TOEIC Test

1. **Close your Eyes!**

2. **Breathe!**

   - *Breathe through your nose*

   - *Hold your breath inside for 3 seconds*

   - *Breath out slowly through your mouth or nose*

   - *Repeat 3 times*

3. **Visualize Beautiful Nature.**

If you are feeling tired during the Listening Section, close your eyes while the Test Narrator is giving directions and breathe deeply.

Test Center Procedures and Regulations

- No test taker will be admitted after test materials have been passed out.

- The following things are not allowed in the testing room.

books	*dictionaries*	*pagers*
paper	*notes*	*translators*
rulers	*calculators*	*stereos or radios*
watch alarms	*cell phones*	*stopwatches*
listening devices	*highlighter pens*	*handheld electronic devices*
mechanical pencils	*pens*	*beepers*
recording equipment	*photographic equipment*	

  any other kind of aid that may help you with the test

- You **may not mark or underline words** in the test book or make notes in the test book or on the answer sheet.

- There is **no scheduled break** during the TOEIC test.

- You must have the supervisor's permission to leave the testing room. Any lost time cannot be made up.

- You will be asked to fill out a 20-minute **TOEIC Background Questionnaire** *before* you take the test. Practice filling out the background questionnaire before Test Day.

The most important things to REMEMBER

NO mechanical pencils

NO pens

NO scratch paper

NO stop watches *(you can have a wristwatch on your desk)*

You CANNOT write in the test book *(some test sites do not care, but **some sites do care**)*

You CANNOT take notes *(some test sites do not care, but **some sites do care**)*

You CANNOT have food or drink in the test room

MASTER
PHOTOGRAPHS

Directions for this Part of the TOEIC: In this part of the test, you will hear four statements about each picture in your textbook. After listening to all four statements, you must select the one statement that best describes what you see in the picture. Then find the number of that question on your answer sheet and mark your answer. The statements will be spoken only one time, and are not printed in your test book.

The Photograph Method

1. Predict Main Nouns.

- ASK: What are the Main Nouns in the photo?
- ASK: Which Nouns are the "**center of attention**" or "**focus**" of the photograph?
- Think of possible **Synonyms** of Main Nouns.
- **Pronouns** for people ("he", "she", "they") can be Main Nouns.

2. Predict Main Actions.

- ASK: What are the Main Nouns **clearly doing**?
- Ignore **Minor Actions** in the photo.

3. Predict Relationships & Locations.

- ASK: What is the **location** the photo was taken?
- ASK: Where are the Main Nouns in **relation to other Nouns**?
- Background Nouns give many **Location** and **Inference Clues**.

4. Predict Conditions.

- ASK: What **adjectives best describe** the Main Nouns?
- ASK: **For Photos with no People:** Are the Main Nouns in the picture *organized* or *disorganized*?

5. Listen to the Statements & Eliminate Tricks.

- ASK: What is wrong with each Answer Choice?
- All Answer Choices are **grammatically correct**.

1. Predict Main Nouns.

- ASK: What are the Main Nouns in the photo?
- ASK: Which Nouns are the "**center of attention**" or "**focus**" of the photograph?
- Think of possible **Synonyms** of Main Nouns.
- **Pronouns** for people ("he", "she", "they") can be Main Nouns.

What Nouns can you see in this photo?

Which of those Nouns seem to be important?
(which Nouns are the "center of attention" or "focus")

What Nouns can you see in this photo?

Which of those Nouns seem to be important?
(which Nouns are the "center of attention" or "focus")

TIP

The correct answer will be about one (or more than one) of these Main Nouns.

2. Predict Main Actions.

- ASK: What are the Main Nouns **clearly doing**?
- Ignore **Minor Actions** in the photo.

> **What Verbs are the Main Nouns possibly doing?**

> **Which of those Verbs seem to be most clear?**

> **What Verbs are the Main Nouns possibly doing?**

> **Which of those Verbs seem to be most clear?**

Photographs with no people in them will usually not have any clear Actions. Focus on predicting Adjectives and Prepositions.

TIP

3. Predict Relationships & Locations.

- ASK: What is the **location** the photo was taken?
- ASK: Where are the Main Nouns in **relation to other Nouns**?
- Background Nouns give many **Location** and **Inference Clues**.

> *What is the location of the photograph?*

> *Where are the Main Nouns in relation to each other?*

> *What is the location of the photograph?*

> *Where are the Main Nouns in relation to each other?*

TIP
Listen for Prepositions that clearly do not describe the Main Nouns—they are usually wrong answers.

4. Predict Conditions.

- ASK: What **adjectives best describe** the Main Nouns?
- ASK: **For Photos with no People:** Are the Main Nouns in the picture *organized* or *disorganized*?

> **What words best describe the Main Nouns?**

> **What words best describe the Main Nouns?**

Descriptions of people's emotions can also be used in correct answers, but the emotions must be clearly seen.

5. Listen to the Statements & Eliminate Tricks.

- ASK: What is wrong with each Answer Choice?
- All Answer Choices are **grammatically correct**.

Extreme Inference   *Wrong Action*   *Wrong Relationship or Location*
Similar-Sounding Word   *Wrong Condition*
Topic-Related Word   *Wrong Object*

Create wrong answers for the photographs above

1. Wrong Object   **1. Wrong Object**

2. Wrong Action   **2. Wrong Action**

3. Wrong Relationship or Location   **3. Wrong Relationship or Location**

4. Wrong Condition   **4. Wrong Condition**

5. Similar-Sounding Word   **5. Similar-Sounding Word**

6. Extreme Inference   **6. Extreme Inference**

7. Topic-Related Word   **7. Topic-Related Word**

TIP

Correct answers almost never talk about the past or future.

The Photographs Method Quiz

1. **Predict** _____.

    What are the _____ in the photo?

    ASK: Which Nouns are the _____ or _____ of the photograph?

    Think of possible _____ of Main Nouns.

    _____ for people can be Main Nouns.

2. **Predict** _____.

    ASK: What are the Main Nouns _____?

    Ignore _____ in the photo.

3. **Predict** _____ & _____.

    ASK: What is the _____ the photo was taken?

    ASK: Where are the Main Nouns in relation to _____?

    Background Nouns give many _____ and _____ Clues.

4. **Predict** _____.

    ASK: **For Photos with no People:** Are the Main Nouns in the picture _____ or _____?

5. **Listen to the Statements & _____.**

    ASK: What is _____ with each Answer Choice?

    All Answer Choices are _____.

Answers on Page 17

Photographs Quiz Exercises

- *Download the audio file for this section at:* **http://masterthetoeic.com/2009/12/master-the-toeic-tracks/**
- *The* **Transcripts** *for all Photograph Questions are on* **Page 31.**

Exercise 1: Predicting Answers

Look at the photos on Pages 25-29. Write 2-3 words for each of the following:

> *Main Objects*
> *Main Actions*
> *Relationships & Locations of Main Objects*
> *Conditions/Adjectives*

Compare your answers with your partner and class.

Exercise 2: Answers & Tricks

Listen to the Answer Choices and identify the correct Answer Choice.

Identify what is wrong with the other Answer Choices.

What tricks do you hear?

> *Wrong Object*
> *Wrong Action*
> *Wrong Relationship or Location*
> *Wrong Condition*
> *Similar-Sounding Word*
> *Extreme Inference*
> *Topic-Related Word*

Compare your answers with your partner and class.

Answers to the Photograph Questions Quiz are on Page 30

1.

2.

3.

4.

5.

6.

7.

8.

9.

10.

Answers to Quiz are on Page 30

Photographs Answers

(Quiz, pages 25-29)

1.	B
2.	D
3.	C
4.	A
5.	C
6.	B
7.	D
8.	A
9.	C
10.	C

Photograph Quiz Transcript

1.
(A) The cups are under the glasses.
(B) The cups are lined up on the table.
(C) The meeting is about to begin.
(D) The cups and plates are disorganized.

2.
(A) They are studying for a test.
(B) They are working on a report.
(C) They are sitting at the table.
(D) They are standing next to the table.

3.
(A) The two men are meeting the women on the
    sidewalk.
(B) The buckets are full of water.
(C) The two men are carrying buckets down the
    sidewalk.
(D) The two men are carrying packets.

4.
(A) The man is enjoying a day skiing.
(B) The man does not know how to ski.
(C) The man is skating.
(D) The man is enjoying what he is seeing.

5.
(A) The students are talking to a teacher.
(B) The class is almost finished.
(C) The students are listening to the teacher.
(D) The students are standing behind the table.

6.
(A) The people are on the sidewalk.
(B) The people are riding bicycles.
(C) The people are going to work.
(D) The people are enjoying the weekend.

7.
(A) The man is writing a magazine.
(B) The man's flight is late.
(C) The man not wearing glasses.
(D) The man is reading a magazine.

8.
(A) The office is cluttered.
(B) The office is closed.
(C) The desk is organized.
(D) The file cabinet is empty.

9.
(A) The professor is reaching.
(B) The students are taking a rest.
(C) The professor is giving a lecture.
(D) The students are giving a lecture.

10.
(A) The street is in a desert.
(B) The street is very wide.
(C) The street is deserted.
(D) The streetlamp is burned out.

MASTER
QUESTION-RESPONSES

The Question-Response Method

1. Identify the Question/Statement Type.

- Common types:

why	*where*	*who*	*when*	*opinion*	*request*	*yes/no*
duration	*what action*	*method*	*choice*	*statement*	*amount*	

- Pay attention to the **first 1-2 words** of the Question to identify the Question Type.
- Some words that identify the Question Type may be in the **middle of a Question**.
- **Tag-Questions** are Yes/No Questions.

2. Decide what the Question is asking.

- Listen for Key Words that give the **Subject**, **Object**, **Topic** and **Action**.
- Listen for **Negative Words** in the Question.
- Listen for the **Verb Tense**.
- Responses to **Tag-Questions** must **answer the main statement** appropriately, *NOT* the tag-question.

3. Listen to Responses and Eliminate Tricks.

- Correct Responses **don't normally repeat key words** unless asking for clarification.
- Some correct Responses are only related to the question by **Context**.

1. Identify the Question/Statement Type.

- Common types:

why	*where*	*who*	*when*	*opinion*	*request*	*yes/no*
duration	*what action*	*method*	*choice*	*statement*	*amount*	

- Pay attention to the **first 1-2 words** of the Question to identify the Question Type.
- Some words that identify the Question Type may be in the **middle of a Question**.
- **Tag-Questions** are Yes/No Questions.

Match the Questions to the correct Question Type (Answers on Page 38)

_____1. Who is your supervisor?   (A) Amount

_____2. What did you do yesterday?   (B) Choice

_____3. Can you open the door for me, please?   (C) Duration

_____4. Why didn't you apply for your current position?   (D) Method

_____5. What do you think about the new boss?   (E) Request

_____6. Will you come Wednesday or Thursday?   (F) Statement

_____7. How did you get to work?   (G) What Action

_____8. How long are you going to stay in Tokyo?   (H) When / What time

_____9. Where were you yesterday?   (I) Where

_____10. How much paper will we need to buy?   (J) Who

_____11. Is this computer working?   (K) Why

_____12. Hey, the printer is out of ink.   (L) Yes/No

_____13. What time does the train leave?   (M) Opinion

Answers on Page 38

What Type of Question is this? How do you know?

14.   "When the boss gets here, can you take her to the meeting?"

What Type of Question is this at first? What Type of Question is it really?

15.   "Do you want to go to the store tomorrow or today?"

Answer on Page 38

Around 1/3 of all wrong Responses are wrong because they are Responses to a different Question Type.

2. Decide what the Question is asking.

- Listen for Key Words that give the **Subject**, **Object**, **Topic** and **Action**.
- Listen for **Negative Words** in the Question.
- Listen for the **Verb Tense**.
- Responses to **Tag-Questions** must **answer the main statement** appropriately, *NOT* the tag-question.

What is the Object?

What is the Subject?

What is the Topic?

What is the Action?

16. "What are you going to do after the meeting?"

17. "Did you fix the copier yesterday?"

18. "How did you arrive at the conference so quickly?"

19. "When you get to the office, can you call me?"

20. "Who do we need to send to the Cincinnati branch office?"

Suggested Answers on Page 38

Tag Questions

What is a Tag Question? What is its purpose, or 'job'?

Which of these Answer Choices are correct? Why?

21. "These instructions are difficult to understand, aren't they?"

    (A) Yes, they are pretty hard.
    (B) Yes, they are pretty easy.
    (C) No, they are pretty hard.
    (D) No, they are pretty easy.

Answer on Page 38

Some Yes/No questions CAN be answered without a "Yes" or "No".

3. Listen to Responses and Eliminate Tricks.
   - Correct Responses **don't normally repeat key words** unless asking for clarification.
   - Some correct Responses are only related to the question by **Context**.

> ***What Type of Questions are these? What are the correct answers?***
>
> ***How are the answers different from what you expected?***

22.   "Can you tell me how to get to the station?"

     (A) The train comes every 30 minutes.
     (B) I am too tired to walk to the station.
     (C) I'm not sure. I'm a stranger here.

23.   "Will you get me the notebook over there?"

     (A) Yes, it is pretty notable.
     (B) Do you mean the red notebook?
     (C) No, I will.

Answers on Page 38

Question-Response Tricks

Similar-Sounding Words
Topic-Related /Wrong Topic
Word Repetition
Wrong Question Type
Wrong Subject/Object
Wrong Verb Tense

> ***Match the Trick to each Answer Choice below***

Question: "Can you drive the boss to tomorrow's meeting?"

____24. *It's at the branch office.*   (A) Similar-Sounding Words

____25. *Yes, I drove him to the meeting.*   (B) Topic-Related / Wrong Topic

____26. *I don't know when the bus leaves.*   (C) Word Repetition

____27. *The meeting was very informative.*   (D) Wrong Question Type

____28. *I'm not sure when the meeting begins.*   (E) Wrong Subject/Object

____29. *She would be happy to.*   (F) Wrong Verb Tense

Answers on Page 38

> If you miss a response, keep listening. If you are able to eliminate the other two responses, you can still get the correct answer.

The Question-Response Method Quiz

1. **Identify the _____.**

   Common types:

   1_____   5_____   8_____   11_____
   2_____   6_____   9_____   12_____
   3_____   7_____   10_____   13_____
   4_____

   Pay attention to the _____ words of the Question.

   Tag-Questions are _____ Questions.

2. **Decide _____.**

   Listen for Key Words that give the _____, _____, _____ and
   _____.

   Listen for _____ words in the Question.

   Listen for the Verb _____.

   Responses to Tag-Questions must answer the _____ statement appropriately, not the
   _____.

3. **Listen to Responses and _____.**

   Correct Responses don't normally _____ key words unless asking for _____.

   Some correct Responses are only related to the Question by _____.

Answers on Page 32

Question-Response Quiz Exercises

- *Download the audio file for this section at:* **http://masterthetoeic.com/2009/12/master-the-toeic-tracks/**
- *The **Transcripts** for all Questions are on **Page 39-40.***

Exercise 1: Question Type & Key Words

Identify what Type of Question and any Key Words in the Question.

why	*duration*
where	*method*
who	*amount*
when	*opinion*
what action	*request*
yes/no	*statement*
choice	

Compare your answers with your partner and class.

Exercise 2: Answers & Tricks

Listen to the Question and Responses and identify the correct Answer Choice.

Try to identify any Trick used by a wrong Answer Choice.

Similar-Sounding Words
Topic-Related / Wrong Topic
Word Repetition
Wrong Question Type
Wrong Subject/Object
Wrong Verb Tense

Compare your answers with your partner and class.

Answers to the Question-Response Quiz are on Page 38

Question-Response Answers

(Method, pages 33-35) *(Quiz, page 37)*

1. J
2. G
3. E
4. K
5. M
6. B
7. D
8. C
9. I
10. A
11. L
12. F
13. H
14. Yes/No
15. Choice
16. Subject = you, Object = *nothing*, Action = going to do
Topic = after meeting
17. Subject = you, Object = copier, Action = did fix
Topic = fix copier
18. Subject = you, Object = *nothing*, Action = how arrive
Topic = arrive at conference
19. Subject = you, Object = me, Action = get to office, call
Topic = call
20. Subject = we, Object = who, Action = need to send
Topic = send to branch office
21. A and D
22. C
23. B
24. B
25. F
26. A
27. C
28. D
29. E

11. C
12. B
13. B
14. A
15. B
16. C
17. A
18. C
19. C
20. A
21. B
22. C
23. A
24. B
25. B
26. C
27. A
28. A
29. A
30. B
31. A
32. C
33. A
34. C
35. B
36. A
37. C
38. B
39. A
40. C

Question-Response Quiz Transcript

11.   Where are last year's financial reports?
    (A)   We went to Hawaii.
    (B)   On vacation.
    (C)   In Nancy's office.

12.   Would you be able to help set up for the meeting?
    (A)   Yes, I can meet you.
    (B)   How long will it take? I'm pretty busy.
    (C)   Why do we need a table set up?

13.   What do you think of the new copier?
    (A)   Yes, I'd love some coffee.
    (B)   It's not as easy to use as the old one.
    (C)   I didn't read the newspaper this morning.

14.   Do you want to work late tonight or finish this on the weekend?
    (A)   Let's take care of it today.
    (B)   I worked late last night.
    (C)   I went to work on Saturday.

15.   How long will the flight be?
    (A)   I agree. It sure is long!
    (B)   At least 2 hours.
    (C)   You can take the next flight.

16.   The presentation went well, don't you think?
    (A)   Yes, I think it will.
    (B)   Yes, he was very presentable.
    (C)   Yes, I'm pretty hopeful we got the contract.

17.   Who called while I was out of the office?
    (A)   The branch manager. He wants to talk with you.
    (B)   The R & D department head has the financial report.
    (C)   Yes, I did.

18.   Would you be able to open the store tomorrow?
    (A)   I think they open at 8:00 tomorrow.
    (B)   I'm not sure when they open.
    (C)   Sure, but I don't have a key to get in.

19.   I don't think I'll get this package to the post office before it closes: I'm just too busy.
    (A)   Yes, it's always busy at the post office.
    (B)   The post office closes at 5:00.
    (C)   Do you want me to mail it for you?

20.   Why did you shut down the computer network?
    (A)   I need to install the new printer software.
    (B)   Yes, I did.
    (C)   I don't know why the computer's not working.

21.   What time will the meeting begin?
    (A)   On May 5th.
    (B)   At 8 in the morning.
    (C)   It began at 9:00.

22.   Did you finish the revisions to the Phillips account?
    (A)   I finish lunch at 1:00.
    (B)   Yes, he wants the revisions done soon.
    (C)   Here it is; it took all week to get done!

23.   I'd like to pay by credit card.
    (A)   I'm sorry, but we only take cash.
    (B)   Yes, you can.
    (C)   Its a new platinum visa card.

24.   Will you be able to make it to the Christmas party?
    (A)   I couldn't make it—I was too busy.
    (B)   I'll have to check with my wife to see if we're free.
    (C)   Yes, of course I can help with the party.

25.   What are you going to do after work?
    (A)   I work every day in the evening.
    (B)   I have to pick up my wife at the airport.
    (C)   I went to the grocery store.

26.   Who's going to pick Martha up at the hospital?
    (A)   No, she doesn't need to go to the hospital.
    (B)   Because I got sick.
    (C)   I can't, but I think Gretchen can.

27. Where will the annual conference be held?
    (A) I heard it was a choice between San Diego and
        Los Angeles.
    (B) We need to discuss many things at the
        conference.
    (C) It'll be held during the last weekend of
        September.

28. What happened?
    (A) I got stuck in traffic.
    (B) I'll go to the party.
    (C) Because I got a raise.

29. Why are you waiting here at the front desk?
    (A) I'm meeting Julie here in a few minutes.
    (B) Because I'm waiting here right now.
    (C) I'll be waiting there in an hour.

30. When's the Johnson report going to be ready?
    (A) I'm ready now.
    (B) I'll be done with it by 3:00.
    (C) He'll report to you in the conference room.

31. How long did you work for the government?
    (A) Eight years.
    (B) Yes, I did.
    (C) It takes five minutes to walk to the
        government offices.

32. Where did you work before coming here?
    (A) The store manager.
    (B) I haven't walked here before.
    (C) Nowhere. This is my first job.

33. Who used the printer last?
    (A) Bob did. Why, is it broken again?
    (B) It should last another year.
    (C) I'm not used to it yet.

34. When is the deadline for the conference
    registration?
    (A) I didn't read the headline.
    (B) I hate waiting in line at conferences.
    (C) Next week on the 15th.

35. Was that package sent off yesterday by courier?
    (A) Couriers aren't cheap.
    (B) What package?
    (C) I don't know where the package was sent.

36. Do you want the pamphlets printed in black and
    white or color?
    (A) I don't care. You can decide.
    (B) They were sent out yesterday.
    (C) Yes, I think that's a good idea.

37. What do you think of the new work schedule?
    (A) I didn't know we were scheduled to go to
        New York.
    (B) Sure, let's change the schedule for the job.
    (C) It's better than the last one.

38. Customer service department. This is Tracy. How
    may I help you?
    (A) Yes, you can.
    (B) I'd like to report a faulty product I just
        bought.
    (C) I can wait, thank you.

39. How are you going to finish typing up your speech
    before tomorrow?
    (A) I'll just have to stay here till it's done.
    (B) I'm going to the conference by bus.
    (C) Sorry I can't go, but I'm all tied up right now.

40. What's the name of that used bookstore on Main
    Street?
    (A) I used to go there all the time.
    (B) It's on the corner of 10th and Main.
    (C) I think it's called Powell's Books.

MASTER
SHORT CONVERSATIONS

The Short Conversation Method

1. Scan the Questions for Key Words.

- Look for 2 or 3 Key Words in each Question. Don't look at Answer Choices.
- One of the Key Words should identify the Question Type.

2. Listen for the Main Problem/Issue.

- As you listen, echo silently information that you hear.
  - ➡ use your fingers and hands to keep track of information each speaker gave.

- In every conversation, at least one person:
  - ➡ needs to **solve a problem**
  - ➡ **needs something**
  - ➡ *or* has a **strong opinion** about a topic
- Listen for **Emphasized Words** and to the **Tones of Voice** of each speaker.

3. Listen for Questions and Answers.

- Don't scan the Answer Choices until after the Conversation is finished.
- Try to predict or infer correct answers based on what you heard.

4. Scan Answer Choices for Predictions & Eliminate Tricks.

- Focus on **Key Words** that make each Answer Choice **different from the other 3 Answer Choices**.

1. Scan the Questions for Key Words.

- Look for 2 or 3 Key Words in each Question. Don't look at Answer Choices.
- One of the Key Words should identify the Question Type.

Common Questions Types:

Who	*What*	*What Time*	*When*	*Where*	*Why*
Which	*Duration*	*Amount*	*Inference*	*Method*	*Opinion*

Deciding Which Questions to listen for

Underline Key Words in the Questions

What Types of Questions are they?

1. According to the man, what is wrong with the computer?

   (A) Its hard drive is damaged
   (B) It needs more memory
   (C) It has a virus
   (D) It is missing important software

2. When will the computer be ready?

   (A) Tomorrow
   (B) Next week
   (C) Later in the day
   (D) 3 days from now

3. What has the man probably already done to try to fix the computer?

   (A) Reinstalled existing software
   (B) Updated old software
   (C) Taken it to a repair center
   (D) Asked a colleague to fix it

Look at the Questions and Answer Choices above.

Which of Questions will be easiest to listen for? Why?

 TIP Listen for and look for Negative Words ("no", "not", "can't", "won't", etc.) in the Conversations, Questions and Answer Choices.

2. Listen for the Main Problem/Issue.

- As you listen, echo silently information that you hear.
  - ➡ use your fingers and hands to keep track of information each speaker gave.

- In every conversation, at least one person:
  - ➡ needs to **solve a problem**
  - ➡ **needs something**
  - ➡ *or* has a **strong opinion** about a topic
- Listen for **Emphasized Words** and to the **Tones of Voice** of each speaker.

Conversation 1

Underline each piece of information spoken by each speaker.

What is the main problem or issue?

Woman:	*Good morning, sir. Are you checking in?*
Man:	*Yes, but I can't seem to find my reservation number.*
Woman:	*That's no problem. If you can provide me with some photo ID and a credit card I'm sure I can find you in our system.*
Man:	*Great! For a minute there I thought I would have to reserve a second room.*

Did the other person help them?

Conversation 2

Underline each piece of information spoken by each speaker.

What is the main problem or issue?

Man:	*Can you help me with this report? I'm having a hard time formatting it.*
Woman:	*Well, I don't know much about that program you're using, but Robert might be more help. He's great at making documents look their best.*
Man:	*Thanks! I'll give him a call right now. My deadline for it is tomorrow's meeting.*
Woman:	*Oh no, that reminds me—I need to print my report for a meeting in an hour!*

Did the other person help them?

3. Listen for Questions and Answers.

- Don't scan the Answer Choices until after the Conversation is finished.
- Try to predict or infer correct answers based on what you heard.

> **What words help you identify Inference Questions?**

infer	*might*	*probably*	*most likely*
imply	*may*	*probable*	*could*

To help you answer Inference Questions, ask yourself:

> **What is the likely relationship between the two speakers?**
>
> **What do the two speakers feel about the topic of the conversation?**

Man: *Learning this new accounting software is taking forever. I'm just too old to learn this.*

Woman: *What do you mean? You were able to figure out how to use that new projector last year. Don't give up—it's hard for anyone to learn a complicated new program.*

Man: *I know. It just feels like every year I have to relearn my job. Why can't we pick one kind of software to use here and stick with it?*

Woman: *We need to keep up with new industry standards and regulations—our old software is outdated.*

> **What is the emotion of each Answer Choice?**
>
> **What are the correct Answers?**

---

4.   How does the man feel about the new software?

    (A) He is happy to learn it
    (B) It is too old
    (C) He wants to stick with it for another year
    (D) It is very difficult to understand

5.   How does the woman feel about the new software?

    (A) She does not understand what it does
    (B) It is necessary for their work
    (C) It is outdated
    (D) It is similar to the projector software

Answers on Page 54

> Answers will not always be heard in the same order as the questions appear on the page. Choose which Questions to listen for-- ignore the rest.

4. Scan Answer Choices for Predictions & Eliminate Tricks

• Focus on **Key Words** that make each Answer Choice **different from the other 3 Answer Choices.**

Underline Key Words in each Answer Choices which make them different from the others

---

Woman: *Good morning, sir. Are you checking in?*

Man: *Yes, but I can't seem to find my reservation number.*

Woman: *That's no problem. If you can provide me with some photo ID and a credit card I'm sure I can find you in our system.*

Man: *Great! For a minute there I thought I would have to reserve a second room.*

Man: *Excuse me, I'm looking for a copy machine which can do both color and black and white.*

Woman: *Well, we have a number of great models for you to choose from. We just got this one in—the Tri-Hue X3. We've received great feedback from people who've bought it.*

Man: *Hmm, I hope its user manual is easy to read—the last machine I bought was really complicated.*

---

6. Where is this conversation probably taking place?

   (A) A conference check-in counter
   (B) A hotel front desk
   (C) A corporate front lobby
   (D) A museum ticket office

7. What was the man worried about?

   (A) He thought he might have lost his photo ID
   (B) He might not have made a reservation
   (C) He reserved a second room
   (D) He would need to purchase a second room

8. What does the woman need from the man?

   (A) Photo identification and credit card
   (B) Picture ID and reservation number
   (C) A hotel room
   (D) A check

9. Where does the conversation most likely take place?

   (A) An auto repair shop
   (B) A coffee shop
   (C) A photographer's studio
   (D) An office supply store

10. What is the man looking to buy?

    (A) A coffee machine
    (B) A video camera
    (C) A copier
    (D) A user manual

11. What does the woman say about the Tri-Hue X3?

    (A) It is not the latest model
    (B) It has an extended warranty
    (C) Past customers have praised it
    (D) It does not print in color

Answers on Page 54

If you look at Answer Choices while listening, it may be difficult to listen effectively; wait till after the Conversation to look at Answer Choices.

Short Conversation Tricks

Extreme Inference
Incorrect Paraphrase
Similar-Sounding Word
Similar Tone
Topic-Related /Wrong Topic
Wrong Detail
Wrong Person

Sample Short Conversation *(use this for understanding the Tricks below)***:**

Man:	*"Can you help me with this report? I'm having a hard time formatting it."*
Woman:	*"Well, I don't know much about that program you're using, but Robert might be more help. He's great at making documents look their best. He knows how to fix reports up quick."*
Man:	*"Thanks! I'll give him a call right now. My deadline for it is tomorrow's meeting."*
Woman:	*"Oh no, that reminds me—I need to print my report for a meeting in an hour!"*

Match the Trick to each Answer Choice below

Question: "Why is the woman not able to help the man with his report?"

_____12. She needs to print a report.   (A) Extreme Inference

_____13. She thinks the copier is broken.   (B) Incorrect Paraphrase

_____14. She formatted a previous report incorrectly.   (C) Similar-Sounding Word

_____15. She is calling Robert right now.   (D) Similar Tone

_____16. She has a hard time formatting her report.   (E) Topic-Related

_____17. She doesn't like using a particular program.   (F) Wrong Detail

_____18. She doesn't know how to fax the report.   (G) Wrong Person

Answers on Page 54

The Short Conversation Method Quiz

1. **Scan the _____ for Key Words.**

    Look for _____ Key Words in each Question.

    Don't look at _____.

    One of the Key Words should identify the _____.

2. **Listen for the _____.**

    - As you listen, _____ information that you hear.

        ➡ use your _____ to keep track of information each speaker gave.

        In every conversation, at least one person:

        ➡ Needs to _____,

        ➡ Needs _____,

        ➡ or has a _____ about a topic.

        Listen for _____ and to the _____ of each speaker.

3. **Listen for Questions and Answers.**

    Don't _____ until after the Conversation is finished

    Try to _____ correct answers based on what you heard

4. **Scan Answer Choices for Predictions & Eliminate Tricks**

    Focus on _____ that make each Answer Choice _____.

Answer on Page 41

Short Conversation Quiz Exercises

- *Download the audio file for this section at:* **http://masterthetoeic.com/2009/12/master-the-toeic-tracks/**
- *The **Transcripts** for all Questions are on **Page 55-56**.*

Exercise 1: Question & Answer Choice Key Words

Underline the Key Words in each Question and Answer Choice.

> **Example:**
>
> Which flight is she taking?
>
> (A)   The one to San Francisco
> (B)   The midnight flight
> (C)   The first flight tomorrow morning
> (D)   The one to Seattle

For each Text, decide which Questions you will listen for, and which Questions you will wait to look at until after the Conversation is finished.

Exercise 2: Listening for Main Ideas & Inferences

After listening to the Short Conversation, answer the following Questions:

- *What is the relationship between the two speakers?*
- *What is the main problem or topic being discussed?*

Compare your answers with your partner and class.

Exercise 3: Answers & Tricks

Try to identify the correct Answer Choice.

Try to identify any Trick used by a wrong Answer Choice.

Extreme Inference	**Topic-Related / Wrong Topic**
Incorrect Paraphrase	**Wrong Detail**
Similar-Sounding Word	**Wrong Person**
Similar Tone	

Compare your answers with your partner and class.

Answers to the Short Conversation Quiz are on Page 54

41.   What is the man formatting?

(A) A news report
(B) A computer program
(C) A professor's paper
(D) A financial report

42.   What is Robert good at doing?

(A) He is good at taking a rest
(B) He is good at formatting programs
(C) He is great at making a mess
(D) He formats documents well

43.   When does the man need the document done?

(A) Earlier that day
(B) Tomorrow
(C) This afternoon
(D) In one hour

44.   Why is the woman confused?

(A) She didn't read a memo sent last week
(B) She didn't receive a memo today
(C) She doesn't know what website to visit
(D) She doesn't understand a computer program

45.   How does one use the new invoice filing system?

(A) Go to the home office
(B) Ask the man to access a program
(C) Go to a website and log into a program
(D) Send a message to the home office

46.   What is probably true?

(A) The man works in the home office
(B) The man read the memo sent last week
(C) The old invoice filing system was confusing
(D) The new invoice filing system is confusing

47.   Why does the man need certain paper supplies?

(A) He needs to restock the supply room
(B) He is going to send out a mass mailing
(C) He needs to send a letter overseas
(D) He is conducting an inventory

48.   What does the woman recommend to the man?

(A) Ask a coworker if he has any extra paper and envelopes
(B) Order more paper and envelopes
(C) Ask Michael to send the letter for him
(D) Send an email instead of a letter

49.   What does the man think happened to the box of paper supplies?

(A) It was sent to China
(B) A client took it
(C) The woman took it
(D) Michael took it

50.   Why is the woman upset?

(A) No one is replying to a survey
(B) They are not making enough money selling their products
(C) They don't have enough products to sell
(D) They don't have many past customers

51.   Why does the man recommend not increasing advertising?

(A) There may be another reason for low sales
(B) More ads will not solve the problem
(C) They do not have enough money now
(D) Their ads are terrible

52.   What does the man recommend?

(A) Increase money spent on online advertising
(B) Send out a survey in the mail
(C) Conduct a survey over the internet
(D) Create more products to sell

53.   Why is the woman not ready for the meeting?

        (A) The office is under reconstruction
        (B) She needs to gather more files
        (C) The photocopier does not work
        (D) She accidently deleted her report

54.   According to the woman, what can the man do to help her?

        (A) Gather files for her report
        (B) Type her report
        (C) Attend the meeting for her in the afternoon
        (D) Help photocopy the report later

55.   When will the woman present her report?

        (A) Today after lunch
        (B) An hour
        (C) In two hours
        (D) Tomorrow in the afternoon

56.   Why is the woman waiting for a call from Computer City?

        (A) She wants to know about the man's computer
        (B) She wants to know about her computer
        (C) She wants to buy a computer
        (D) She wants to copy a disk

57.   Why is the woman worried about losing the files on her computer?

        (A) She needs them to cure a virus
        (B) There were company files on the hard drive
        (C) There were important files on the hard drive
        (D) She needs them to make a phone call

58.   What did Sam say was ready to be picked up at Computer City?

        (A) A disk
        (B) Her computer
        (C) A new computer
        (D) A hard drive

59.   Why did Frank call Ms. Williams?

        (A) To place an order
        (B) To inform the woman about a completed project
        (C) To ask about a delivery he is expecting
        (D) To set up a shipment

60.   Why did Frank probably not know what he needed for the delivery?

        (A) A salesperson filled out the P.O. incorrectly
        (B) Ms. Williams did not fill out a P.O.
        (C) Ms. Williams filled out the P.O. incorrectly
        (D) Ms. Williams changed her mind

61.   What day does Ms. Williams say she wants the bookcase and desk delivered?

        (A) Today
        (B) Tomorrow
        (C) Thursday
        (D) Friday

62.   Why does the woman want to talk with Peter?

        (A) She is making a report on his trip
        (B) She wants him to take a business trip
        (C) She thinks he filled out a report wrong
        (D) She wants to give him a reimbursement check

63.   Why does the woman think the expense report is wrong?

        (A) Peter didn't turn it in on time
        (B) Some items on the report are illegal
        (C) Some items on the report aren't reimbursable expenses
        (D) Peter turned the report in to the wrong office

64.   How does Peter explain his high dinner expenses?

        (A) He didn't know how much the meals cost
        (B) He was eating at expensive places
        (C) He was dining with his wife
        (D) He was treating company clients

65.   Why does the man have to leave?

        (A) He needs to meet campus security
        (B) He has a medical appointment
        (C) He needs to buy a new cell phone
        (D) He needs to attend a meeting

66.   What will Rachel do later today?

        (A) Go on a date
        (B) Call campus security
        (C) Pick up her parking permit
        (D) Clean the house

67.   Why does the man want Rachel to be at the house?

        (A) He wants to go to dinner with her
        (B) He is expecting a delivery
        (C) He wants her to set up an appointment
        (D) He is expecting a call

68.   When did the man last talk with the IT department?

        (A) Last weekend
        (B) Yesterday
        (C) Today
        (D) A week ago

69.   What does the man think of the new website?

        (A) It is slower than the current one
        (B) It is better than the current one
        (C) It has too many features
        (D) It has too few pages

70.   According to the man, why is the website not yet ready?

        (A) It does not run smoothly
        (B) There are some links that need to be fixed
        (C) The IT department needs to add more pages
        (D) The IT department needs to add more customer features

Answers to the Short Conversation Quiz are on Page 54

Short Conversations Answers

(Method, pages 41-46)

1. what
2. when
3. inference
4. D
5. B
6. B
7. D
8. A
9. D
10. C
11. C
12. F
13. E
14. G
15. B
16. A
17. D
18. C

(Quiz, pages 49-53)

41.	D	56.	B
42.	D	57.	C
43.	B	58.	A
44.	A	59.	B
45.	C	60.	A
46.	B	61.	B
47.	C	62.	C
48.	A	63.	C
49.	D	64.	D
50.	B	65.	B
51.	A	66.	A
52.	C	67.	D
53.	D	68.	B
54.	D	69.	B
55.	A	70.	B

Short Conversation Quiz Transcript

Questions 41 through 43 refer to the following conversation

Man: Can you help me with this financial report? I'm having a hard time formatting it.

Woman: Well, I don't know much about that program you're using, but Robert might be more help. He's great at making documents look their best. He helped me with my report this morning.

Man: Thanks! I'll give him a call right now. My deadline for it is tomorrow's meeting.

Woman: Oh no, that reminds me—I still need to print my report for a meeting in an hour!

Questions 44 through 46 refer to the following conversation

Woman: I don't get this memo we just got from the home office. It says that starting next month we'll need to file all invoices with them before filling any orders.

Man: Didn't you read the e-mail they sent out last week? They told everyone about the new online invoice filing system.

Woman: A new online program? No, I must have missed that message.

Man: It looks pretty simple. We just have to enter all the information via our website. Here, let me show you how to log on to it.

Questions 47 through 49 refer to the following conversation

Man: I need to send an official letter to one of our clients in China, but it looks like we are out of letterhead and our business envelopes.

Woman: Are you sure? I saw a whole box of both the paper and envelopes in the supply room last week.

Man: I saw it, too, last week, but I remember Michael mentioning a mass mailing he needed to do.

Woman: If that's the case, you should ask him if he has any extras—you only need one of each, right?

Questions 50 through 52 refer to the following conversation

Woman: Our sales figures are terrible! We need to spend more time and money on advertising.

Man: But more ad time will not necessarily mean more sales. I think we should do a little research to find out if it's more than just lack of exposure.

Woman: True. What do you recommend?

Man: Let's send out an email survey to all our past customers to find out how they first heard about us, and why they bought our products. Then we'll have a better idea of how to increase our sales.

Questions 53 through 55 refer to the following conversation

Man: Hi Sara. What are you working on? Are you ready for this afternoon's meeting?

Woman: Oh, hi. No, I'm way behind. Can you believe I accidently deleted the entire report—I've been spending the last two hours reconstructing it.

Man: Really? Is there anything I can do? Can I help you gather any more files? I'm a pretty fast typist.

Woman: Thanks, but I don't think there's anything you can do right now, but if you come back in an hour you can help me photocopy the report.

Questions 56 through 58 refer to the following conversation

Woman: Have we received a call from Sam at Computer City yet?

Man: Yeah, but he said your computer is infected with a virus. He had to completely erase your hard drive.

Woman: He deleted everything? But we had all of our family photos and all my music on it.

Man: Don't worry. He said that he downloaded everything he could onto a disk. If you want, you can go pick it up at his shop.

Questions 59 through 61 refer to the following conversation

Man: Hi, Ms. Williams? This is Frank from Custom Cabinets. The bookcase and desk you ordered are finished and ready to be picked up.

Woman: Thank you for calling. I've been hoping to hear from you since yesterday. However, I thought you would be delivering them to us.

Man: Did you have that on your order? One of our sales reps must have forgotten to put that down on the Purchase Order. Would Thursday or Friday be okay?

Woman: Actually, we were hoping to have it before then. Can you deliver them tomorrow?

Questions 62 through 64 refer to the following conversation

Woman: Can I see you for a minute, Peter? I wanted to discuss the expense report you filed last week.

Man: Sure. Was there something wrong with the report?

Woman: There were a few you listed which are a little excessive, like the amount you spent on dinners. Over $50 a meal! And we don't cover hotel snack bars.

Man: Oh, I see. Maybe I didn't explain them enough on the report. Those dinners were with clients, so I'm pretty sure everything I covered was a legitimate expense.

Questions 65 through 67 refer to the following conversation

Man: Hey, Rachel, are you going to be the house for a while, or are you heading out with your friends today? I have to step out of a couple hours.

Woman: No, I'll be here, at least till dinnertime—I've got a date with Steve. Why? What's up?

Man: Well, I have a doctor's appointment this afternoon, but I'm also expecting a call from campus security. They said they would tell me if my parking permit would be ready to be picked up.

Woman: Sure. I'll give you a call as soon as I find out if it's ready.

Questions 68 through 70 refer to the following conversation

Woman: Have you talked to the IT Department today about when the new website will be ready?

Man: No, but I did touch base with them yesterday. They were trying to fix a few links, but said everything should be done by this weekend.

Woman: That's good to hear—they are already a week past schedule. Have you seen what it looks like?

Man: A little. Overall, the design is really nice, and it runs much smoother than our current one. They've added a lot of great new features which I think will make it nicer for customers, too.

MASTER
SHORT TALKS

Directions for this Part of the TOEIC: In this part of the test, you will hear some talks given by a single speaker. You will be asked to answer three questions about what the speaker says in each talk. Select the best response to each question and mark the letter (A), (B), (C) or (D) on your answer sheet. The talks will not be printed in your test book and will be spoken only one time.

The Short Talk Method

1. **Scan the Questions for Key Words.**

   - Look for **2-3 Key Words** in each Question. Don't look at Answer Choices.
   - One of the Key Words should **identify the Question Type**.
   - If the Question asks "which is true/said" or "which is NOT true/said", look at the Answer Choices as soon as possible.

2. **Listen for Key Words from Questions.**

   - When you hear Key Words for a Question, begin to **Scan that Question's Answer Choices**.
   - Wait to answer **Inference, Topic or Purpose Questions** after the Talk.

3. **Listen to Questions and Scan Answer Choices.**

   - Don't bubble while listening to the talk.
   - Focus on **Key Words** that make each Answer Choice **different from the other 3 Answer Choices**.

1. Scan the Questions for Key Words.

- Look for **2-3 Key Words** in each Question. Don't look at Answer Choices.
- One of the Key Words should **identify the Question Type**.
- If the Question asks "which is true/said" or "which is NOT true/said", look at the Answer Choices as soon as possible.

Common Questions Types:

Who	*What*	*Why*	*Which*	*Where*	*What time/When*
How long	*How much*	*Method*	*Purpose*	*Topic*	*Inference*

Deciding Which Questions to listen for

Circle Key Words in the Questions

Identify each Type of Question

1.   What is the goal of the speech?

   (A) To announce a marketing campaign
   (B) To award a colleague
   (C) To celebrate reaching a sales goal
   (D) To welcome a new staff member

2.   Why did the company have difficulties in its first year?

   (A) Lack of funding
   (B) Only one store
   (C) An accident in its warehouse
   (D) Too few trained staff

3.   What is the company now known for?

   (A) Customer satisfaction
   (B) Technological inventions
   (C) Effective overseas marketing projects
   (D) Innovative sales techniques

Answers on Page 70

Which Questions will be easiest to listen for? Why?

2. Listen for Key Words from Questions.

- When you hear Key Words for a Question, begin to **Scan that Question's Answer Choices**.
- Answer **Inference, Topic or Purpose Questions** after the Talk.

Types of Short Talks:

Introductory speech	*Passenger announcement*	*News report*	*Phone message*
Advertisement	*Store announcement*	*Business report*	*Automated message*
Meeting speech	*Public service announcement*		

Talk 1

What type of Talk is this?

Please be advised that the passenger elevator to platform 3 is not in service at this time.
Passengers with disabilities who need to go to that platform can use the street-level causeways to reach either platform 1 or 2, both of which connect to platform 3. Passengers may also ask any station staff person to help them use one of our staff-only elevators. All other passengers may still reach platform 3 via the main stairway from the central ticket office. If this technical issue causes you to miss your train we will be happy to help you reserve another seat on a later departure. We regret any inconvenience this may cause you and are working on restoring direct elevator service to platform 3 as soon as possible.

Where would this Talk be heard?

Who are they talking to?

What details are similar to other details in the Talk?

Talk 2

What type of Talk is this?

Good afternoon ladies and gentlemen. Before we break up into different discussion groups, I would like to take a minute to talk about how today will go. The first two hours we have six rooms set up for six different panel discussions. You will want to attend one panel for the first hour then switch to another room to listen to another panel. Next will be a brief lunch break—there are various food carts outside the hotel with a lot of delicious choices. We'll start the afternoon sessions promptly at 1:00 p.m. As with the morning discussion panels, you can move to a new panel every hour, which means that by the end of the day you should be able to attend all the panels we have set up for today. Alright, if there are no questions, please make your way to one of the panel rooms.

Where would this Talk be heard?

Who are they talking to?

What details are similar to other details in the Talk?

Listen for emphasized words. Emphasized words can often point towards important pieces of information to help you choose correct answers.

3. Listen to Questions and Scan Answer Choices.
- Don't bubble while listening to the talk.
- Focus on **Key Words** that make each Answer Choice **different from the other 3 Answer Choices**.

What words make these Answer Choices different from each other?

4.   What cities does the tour go to?

    (A) London, Paris, Berlin, Moscow
    (B) London, Paris, Oslo, Rome
    (C) London, Madrid, Oslo, Rome
    (D) London, Dublin, Athens, Rome

5.   What does the man need?

    (A) A fax number and credit card
    (B) A fax number and check
    (C) A phone number and check
    (D) Photo ID and a credit card

Use the Questions and Answer Choices to predict correct answers

Which Answer Choices support or complement Answer Choices in other Questions?

6.   Who is speaking?

    (A) A foreign ambassador
    (B) A teacher assistant
    (C) A university president
    (D) A company CEO

7.   Where does Mrs. Thule work?

    (A) At an employment center
    (B) At a governmental research center
    (C) At a non-profit organization
    (D) At a stock investment company

8.   What will happen next?

    (A) A package will be delivered
    (B) An award will be given
    (C) A treaty will be signed
    (D) A class will begin

TIP Answers will not always be heard in the same order as the questions appear on the page. Choose which Questions to listen for-- ignore the rest.

How to answer Topic & Purpose & Inference Questions

What type of Talk is this?

Over the last 2 weeks, with falling temperatures and home heating costs rising, city officials are reaching out to the public to ask for support for the neediest citizens of our fair city. Local food shelters are asking all citizens to open their hearts to the thousands of their homeless and poor neighbors and donate canned food, warm clothes and toys and make this holiday season a time of joy for everyone living here. You can donate directly to any local food shelter or charity-run store, or bring any donations to our lobby here at our station. If you have any questions about how to help, don't hesitate to call into our program— we'll be devoting the next hour talking to the city mayor, who is here in the studio to talk more about what the food shelters need and answer any questions our callers might have.

Where would this Talk be heard?

Who is talking?

Who are they talking to?

9.   What kind of announcement is this?

(A) A request for donations
(B) An announcement of a mayoral election
(C) A request for callers
(D) A announcement of a new program

10.   Who is the likely audience of this announcement?

(A) Poor families
(B) Radio announcers
(C) Food shelters
(D) City populace

11.   When would you likely hear this announcement?

(A) Spring
(B) Summer
(C) Fall
(D) Winter

Answers on Page 70

How to identify Inference Questions

What is an Inference Question?

infer	*might*	*probably*	*most likely*
imply	*may*	*probuble*	*could*

Listen for and look for Negative Words in the Talks, Questions and Answer Choices.

TIP

Short Talks Tricks

Extreme Inference
Incorrect Paraphrase
Similar Types of Detail
Topic-Related /Wrong Topic
Wrong Detail

Sample Short Talk *(use this for understanding the Tricks below)***:**

> **Woman:**   *Good afternoon ladies and gentlemen. I would like to introduce you to the keynote speaker of this year's sales conference. Daniel Oliveri has been a leading voice in the field of online-marketing over the last four years, developing many innovative strategies which have become industry standards. Before this, Mr. Oliveri spent a decade in the field of webpage design, working for Apple Computers, building websites that were user-friendly, rich in content, artistically designed, and providing companies with information to help them better serve their customers. Tonight he will be speaking on the theme of this conference: how to create a 5-step plan to draw potential customers to your website through online advertising. Everyone, please join me in welcoming Daniel Oliveri.*

Match the Trick to each Question & Answer Choice below

_____12. How long did Mr. Oliveri design web pages?   (A) Extreme Inference
     (A) 14 years

_____13. What did Mr. Oliveri create at Apple?   (B) Incorrect Paraphrase
     (A) A 5-step plan for online ads

_____14. How long did Mr. Oliveri design web pages?   (C) Similar Types of Detail
     (A) Four years

_____15. What will Mr. Oliveri talk about?   (D) Topic-Related / Wrong Topic
     (A) How to become an online customer

_____16. What did Mr. Oliveri do for the last four years?   (F) Wrong Detail
     (A) Speak at sales conferences

Answers on Page 70

The Short Talks Method Quiz

1. Scan the _____ for Key Words.

    Look for _____ in each Question. Don't look at _____.

    One of the Key Words should identify the _____.

    If the Question asks "_____" or "_____", look at the Answer Choices as soon as possible.

2. Listen for _____ from Questions.

    When you hear _____, begin to _____.

    Answer _____, _____ or _____ Questions after the Talk.

3. Listen to _____ and Scan _____

    Don't bubble while _____.

    Focus on _____ that make each Answer Choice _____.

Answers on Page 57

Short Talks Quiz Exercises

- *Download the audio file for this section at:* **http://masterthetoeic.com/2009/12/master-the-toeic-tracks/**
- *The **Transcripts** for all Questions are on **Page 71-72**.*

Exercise 1: Question & Answer Choice Key Words

Circle the Key Words in each Question and Answer Choice.

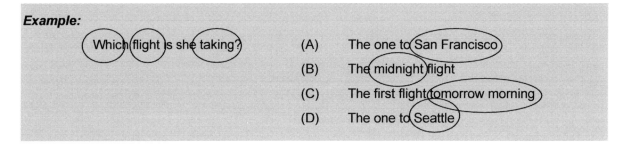

Example:

Which flight is she taking?	(A)	The one to San Francisco
	(B)	The midnight flight
	(C)	The first flight tomorrow morning
	(D)	The one to Seattle

For each Talk, decide which Questions you will listen for, and which Questions you will wait to look at until after the Talk is finished.

Also, identify any **Topic or Purpose Questions.**

Exercise 2: Main Ideas & Inferences

After listening to the Short Talk, answer the following Questions:

- *What Type of Talk is it?*
- *Who is the Talk for?*
- *Where might this Talk be heard?*
- *What information in the Talk is similarly-phrased?*

Compare your answers with your partner and class.

Exercise 3: Answers & Tricks

Try to identify the correct Answer Choice and any Trick used by a wrong Answer Choice.

| *Extreme Inference* | *Topic-Related / Wrong Topic* | *Incorrect Paraphrase* |
| *Wrong Detail* | *Similar-Type of Detail* | |

Compare your answers with your partner and class.

Answers to the Short Talk Quiz are on Page 70

71.   What will Mr. Oliveri talk about?

       (A) How to create a blue-chip company
       (B) People who work at blue-chip companies
       (C) How to speak at sales conferences
       (D) How to use internet advertising

72.   How long did Mr. Oliveri work as a webpage designer?

       (A) 4 years
       (B) 5 years
       (C) 10 years
       (D) 14 years

73.   What does Mr. Oliveri do now?

       (A) Writes books on speaking at conferences
       (B) Creates web pages for Apple Computers
       (C) Creates ads for websites
       (D) Writes books on internet advertising

74.   What was NOT a result of the floods and mudslides?

       (A) Tourists canceled flights to Hawaii
       (B) Bridges were washed out
       (C) People were killed or hurt
       (D) Roads were damaged

75.   How long is it expected to fix the damage caused by the disaster?

       (A) 24 hours
       (B) A week
       (C) About 3 weeks
       (D) Several years

76.   How much money has been raised for victims in Hawaii?

       (A) Only several hundred dollars
       (B) Over two hundred thousand dollars
       (C) Around five million dollars
       (D) More than twenty-four million dollars

77.   What is the main purpose of this talk?

        (A) To ask listeners to sell their gold
        (B) To get listeners to buy gold
        (C) To ask for advice on a good investment
        (D) To inform listeners of the price of gold

78.   What is now causing gold to rise in price?

        (A) The value of the U.S. dollar is lower
        (B) The value of the U.S. dollar is higher
        (C) There are few investors in gold
        (D) There increased gold mining in the U.S.

79.   What must you do in order to begin investing with Goldmasters?

        (A) Call Goldmasters and fill out a questionnaire
        (B) Go to a website and purchase a gold brick
        (C) Go to a website and download a brochure
        (D) Go to a website and fill out a questionnaire

---

80.   What will happen in about 5 minutes?

        (A) Dinner will begin
        (B) The boat will leave the pier
        (C) The boat will arrive at the pier
        (D) Passengers will find a seat

81.   What is probably true?

        (A) Passengers could not leave the forward cabin during the cruise
        (B) It is now after midnight
        (C) There is only one exit ramp on the boat
        (D) The boat finished the cruise at Pier 12

82.   What do passengers probably need to do to get back to their cars?

        (A) Walk south to a parking lot
        (B) Board a boat to another town at Pier 12
        (C) Take a bus to a public parking lot
        (D) Take a taxi to the next town

83.   Why is Sunrise Hotel calling Ms. Kudron?

        (A) To inform her of a necessary change to her reservation
        (B) To confirm her reservation for next month
        (C) To offer her a discount for staying at Sunrise Hotel
        (D) To inform her that Sunrise Hotel is going out of business

84.   Why is Sunrise Hotel closed?

        (A) A new hotel opened across the street
        (B) It suffered a fire earlier in the day
        (C) Its rooms are being renovated
        (D) Its doors will not close properly

85.   What must Ms. Kudron do to change her reservation?

        (A) Call Quality Inn and reserve a room there
        (B) Visit Sunrise Hotel's website
        (C) Find another hotel on her own
        (D) Call Sunrise Hotel before she arrives

---

86.   What is the primary purpose of this talk?

        (A) To give advice on how to travel by subway or train in Japan
        (B) To outline a business trip itinerary
        (C) To plan a trip overseas
        (D) To sign people up for a job fair

87.   How many meetings with study abroad agents have been planned for the trip?

        (A) 2
        (B) 3
        (C) 5
        (D) 7

88.   According to the talk, what is probably true?

        (A) This is the first time these people have taken a business trip to Japan
        (B) There are at least 3 people going on the trip
        (C) The agent meetings are not important
        (D) Only men are going on this trip

89.   What is NOT happening today at Sun Valley Mall?

        (A) A new department store is opening
        (B) Local celebrities are attending an event
        (C) The mall is open for only 2 hours
        (D) A music band is performing in a store

90.   What will people receive for attending the grand opening?

        (A) A coupon for a department store
        (B) A free CD from a jazz band
        (C) A tour with the city mayor
        (D) An interview on the radio

91.   Who is attending the grand opening?

        (A) A local TV personality
        (B) Three musical groups
        (C) A state governor
        (D) A radio show host

92.   What information can you find at Paradise Travel's website?

        (A) A list of extensions for advisors
        (B) Advice on how to run a travel company
        (C) How to contact embassies
        (D) Details about a special travel program

93.   What must you do in order to speak to a specific staff person at Paradise Travel?

        (A) Press 0
        (B) Press 1
        (C) Press 2
        (D) Go to their website

94.   Who would probably want to press 0?

        (A) Someone who wants to book a travel package
        (B) Someone who needs to talk to a particular Paradise Travel staff member
        (C) Someone who already purchased a trip through Paradise Travel
        (D) Someone who wants to become a travel advisor

95.   According to the report, why is the amusement park's attendance low?

        (A) It is now the middle of winter
        (B) Hong Kong residents aren't familiar with Disney's theme park
        (C) There are not enough local ads
        (D) Hong Kong citizens don't enjoy amusement parks

96.   How will Disney try to increase attendance at the theme park?

        (A) Add more rides
        (B) Lower the price of individual tickets
        (C) Offer a free pass for every ticket purchased
        (D) Hire experts to suggest solutions

97.   How does the Hong Kong theme park compare with Disney's other parks?

        (A) There are fewer rides at the Hong Kong park
        (B) There are more rides at the Hong Kong park
        (C) Admissions to the Hong Kong park is more expensive
        (D) The other parks are more attractive

---

98.   What is the purpose of this announcement?

        (A) To report a stolen vehicle
        (B) To report a speeding truck on a highway
        (C) To warn citizens of a possible robbery
        (D) To warn citizens of criminals loose in the city

99.   Which of the following statements is true of the suspected robbers?

        (A) They drove a white truck
        (B) They were last seen heading toward Rochester
        (C) They carried weapons when they entered the bank
        (D) They broke a window to enter the bank

100.   Who should someone call if they see the suspects?

        (A) The police
        (B) 1st National Bank
        (C) The Rochester City Hall
        (D) The Gresham City Hall

Answers to the Short Talk Quiz are on Page 70

Short Talks Answers

(Method, pages 57-62)

1. purpose
2. why
3. what

Questions 4-8 answered in Class Discussions

9.   A
10. D
11. D
12. A
13. F
14. C
15. D
16. B

(Quiz, pages 65-69)

71.	D	86.	B
72.	C	87.	D
73.	D	88.	B
74.	A	89.	C
75.	D	90.	A
76.	B	91.	D
77.	B	92.	D
78.	A	93.	C
79.	D	94.	A
80.	C	95.	B
81.	B	96.	C
82.	A	97.	A
83.	A	98.	D
84.	B	99.	C
85.	D	100.	A

Short Talk Quiz Transcript

Questions 71 through 73 refer to the following speech
"Good afternoon ladies and gentlemen. I would like to introduce you to our keynote speaker of this year's conference. Daniel Oliveri has been a bestselling author in the field of online-marketing over the last four years, developing many innovative strategies which have become industry standards. Before this, Mr. Oliveri spent a decade in the field of webpage design, working for Apple Computers by building websites that were user-friendly, rich in content, artistically designed, and provided Apple with information to help them better serve their customers. Tonight he will be speaking on the theme of this conference: how create a 5-step plan to draw potential customers to your website through online ads."

Questions 74 through 76 refer to the following report
"Torrential rains caused flash floods and mudslides throughout the Hawaiian islands last week, killing over 20 people and injuring several hundred. Many coastal towns and resorts were devastated by raging waters that stormed down from central mountains and took out dozens of roads and bridges in a matter of hours. Damage resulting from the disaster are estimated to be close to $5 million and are expected to take over three years to repair. Donations for victims of the floods and mudslides have been pouring in, with over $200,000 already raised in the last 24 hours. Following the disaster, Hawaii's governor declared a day of mourning to remember the victims."

Questions 77 through 79 refer to the following advertisement
"During these uncertain times, isn't it smart to invest in something that you know will always have value? Gold has been a good investment for a long time, and now a combination of factors, including a weakening U.S. dollar, are driving gold's price even higher. But does that mean it's too late to join the gold rush? Hardly. These days it's easier than ever to invest in gold, so let Goldmasters help you enter this lucrative market and invest wisely. Visit our website, www.goldmasters.com, and complete a short questionnaire regarding your investment goals. You will be contacted by a Goldmaster advisor and join the ranks of smart investors that are using gold to build their future prosperity, one brick at a time."

Questions 80 through 82 refer to the following announcement
"Ladies and gentleman, I hope you have enjoyed tonight's midnight dinner cruise of Astoria Bay and the Columbia River. The ship will be docking in approximately five minutes, so for your safety we ask all guests at this time to find a seat either in the forward cabin or observation deck while we dock. Once we are docked, remember to collect all of your belongings before exiting the ship. All passengers will need to use the main ramp in the rear of the boat. Please note that we are not docking at the same pier we left from, so once you exit the boat, turn left and head south down the boardwalk a quarter mile till you see the Pier 12 and the public parking lot to the right, just past the bus terminal."

Questions 83 through 85 refer to the following message
"This is a message for Lisa Kudron. This is Darian Phelps of Sunrise Hotel in Vancouver, Canada. I'm sorry to bother you at home, but we regret to inform you that Sunrise Hotel suffered from a fire this morning and must close its doors for the next month to undergo repairs. However, we want to offer to help you find alternate lodging for your stay in our city. We have made arrangements with the Quality Inn across the street to take any of our guests—please contact us before your arrival at 1-340-353-6977 to let us know if you want us to book you a room there or receive a full refund for your reservation."

Questions 86 through 88 refer to the following speech
Take a minute to look at the schedule for next week's business trip to Japan. You'll note that unlike last time, I won't be there with you, so you'll want to have this schedule with you to help you find the correct subway and train. Monday and Tuesday will be the job fair, with each of you manning an information booth on three different floors. Wednesday will be meetings with five different study abroad agents, whereas on Thursday you only have two agent meetings. While it is best that you go to the meetings together, it is not necessary for all of you to be at each one. Any questions? No, then have a safe flight, and see you in a week!

Questions 89 through 91 refer to the following announcement

"Attention valued shoppers! Sun Valley Mall would like to inform you that between the hours of 11:00 a.m. and 1:00 p.m. at the South Entrance you will be able to witness the grand opening of our new Macy's department store. Mayor Sean Adams and local radio show personality Tom Potter will be there to cut the ribbon and welcome Macy's first shoppers into the store, with the Barton Trio jazz band performing live in Macy's all afternoon. All shoppers who attend the grand opening will receive a coupon for 25% off any single item purchased in Macy's today. Don't miss out on the exciting event!"

Questions 92 through 94 refer to the following message

"Thank you for calling Paradise Travel. All of our operators are busy at this time. If you are looking for a list of our famous discount vacation packages, please visit us at www.paradisetravel.com. There you will also find information on how to sign up for our Ambassador Tourist program, along with helpful tips for traveling overseas. If you wish to speak with one of our expert travel advisors to help you plan a trip, please press 0 and stay on the line. If you have already booked a travel package with us and need some help, press 1. If you know the extension of a staff member you would like to speak to, press 2 then their extension, followed by the pound key now. "

Questions 95 through 97 refer to the following report

"Disney announced today that attendance is lower than expected at its newest theme park in Hong Kong, but hopes the summer holidays will make up the difference. Marketing experts say that unfamiliarity with Disney's brand and the small size of the park is mainly to blame for the problem--with fewer than 20 attractions, Hong Kong Disney has half the attractions of the company's parks in other countries. A Disney spokesperson acknowledges that the park needs to do well this summer, and will begin a new advertising campaign soon. In addition, Hong Kong residents will receive a second visit free with the purchase of a regular ticket. Disney expects longer-term growth as mainland China becomes more familiar with Disney and its products."

Questions 98 through 100 refer to the following announcement

"Citizens of the cities of Rochester and Gresham are advised to be on the lookout for two individuals wanted in connection with this morning's armed robbery of the downtown branch of 1st National Bank. Authorities report that two men are alleged to have smashed open the doors of the bank before it opened, surprising bank staff. The two individuals, described as white men in their 30's and wearing black overcoats and white tennis shoes, were last seen driving away from the scene of the crime in a red pickup truck, heading east on Highway-84 towards Gresham. If you see anyone fitting this description, do not approach them, but contact the police immediately. Thank you for your assistance."

MASTER
INCOMPLETE SENTENCES

Directions for this Part of the TOEIC: In each question, you will find a word or phrase missing. Four Answer Choices are given below each sentence. You must choose the best answer to complete the sentence. Then mark the letter (A), (B), (C), or (D) on your answer sheet.

The Incomplete Sentence Method

1. **Compare the Answer Choices to identify the Type of Question.**

   - Do most Answer Choices *look similar* but have *different meanings*?   ➡ **Vocabulary** is being tested
   - Do most Answer Choices *look different* but have *similar meanings*?   ➡ **Context** is being tested
   - Do most Answer Choices have the *same root word*?   ➡ **Grammar** is being tested
   - Do most Answer Choices have *conjunctions, participles* or *prepositions*? ➡ **Structure** is being tested
   - Some Questions may test more than one type of issue.
   - Some Answer Choice words can be more than one **Type of Word**.

2. **Look for Clues before and after the Missing Word.**

   - Determine the Part of Speech of the Missing Word by skimming the sentence for **Grammar Clues**.
   - Skim the sentence to understand the **Topic of the Sentence**.
   - Remember that some Missing Words may be a combination of **two different Types of Words**.
   - Eliminate Answer Choices that are not the correct **Type of Word**.

3. **Determine which Answer Choices don't fit with the sentence.**

   - For **Vocabulary Questions**: Ask yourself if Answer Choices fit the **Topic** of the Sentence.
   - For **Context Questions**: Ask yourself if Answer Choices fit the **Topic** of the Sentence.
   - For **Grammar Questions**: Ask yourself if Answer Choices fit the **Verb Tense** of the Sentence.
   - For **Structure Questions**: Determine the **relationship** between the two parts of the sentence.

1. Compare the Answer Choices to identify the Type of Question.

- Do most Answer Choices *look similar* but have *different meanings*?   ➡ **Vocabulary** is being tested
- Do most Answer Choices *look different* but have *similar meanings*?   ➡ **Context** is being tested,
- Do most Answer Choices have the *same root word*?   ➡ **Grammar** is being tested
- Do most Answer Choices have *conjunctions, participles* or *prepositions*? ➡ **Structure** is being tested
- Some Questions may test more than one type of issue.
- Some Answer Choice words can be more than one **Type of Word**.

Types of Words used in the Incomplete Sentence Answer Choices

What do these Types of Words do? What is their 'job' in an English sentence?

Noun	Verb
Adjectives	Adverbs
Prepositions	Conjunctions

Vocabulary Questions

What Types of Words are these?

1. (A) reinvestment
    (B) investigation
    (C) member
    (D) remember

2. (A) limited
    (B) litigation
    (C) literal
    (D) liability

Context Questions

What Types of Words are these?

Which Answer Choices have <u>similar</u> meanings? How are they different?

Which Answer Choices have <u>opposite</u> meanings?

3. (A) high
    (B) tall
    (C) deep
    (D) depth

4. (A) far from
    (B) on
    (C) near
    (D) by

To study more about Types of Words, go to
http://www.southampton.liunet.edu/academic/pau/course/websuf.htm.

Grammar Questions

What Types of Words are these?

5. (A) remembered
   (B) remember
   (C) forget
   (D) forgettable

6. (A) schedule
   (B) scheduling
   (C) scheduled
   (D) schedulable

Structure Questions

What Types of Words are these?

Which Answer Choices have <u>similar</u> meanings? How are they different?

Which Answer Choices have <u>opposite</u> meanings?

7. (A) look at
   (B) look
   (C) within
   (D) look within

8. (A) due to
   (B) caused
   (C) resulted in
   (D) because

Identify the Types of Question for each set of Answer Choices below

9. (A) diagnose
   (B) diagnosed
   (C) diagnosing
   (D) diagnosis

12. (A) quickly
    (B) rapid
    (C) sluggish
    (D) carefully

10. (A) written
    (B) rote
    (C) informational
    (D) spoken

13. (A) receptive
    (B) reservation
    (C) received
    (D) receipt

11. (A) under
    (B) over
    (C) above
    (D) beneath

14. (A) have been taken
    (B) has taken
    (C) is taking
    (D) takes

Remember that Gerunds can look like verbs or adjectives.

TIP

2. Look for Clues before and after the Missing Word.
- Determine the Part of Speech of the Missing Word by skimming the sentence for **Grammar Clues**.
- Skim the sentence to understand the **Topic of the Sentence**.
- Remember that some Missing Words may be a combination of **two different Types of Words**.
- Eliminate Answer Choices that are not the correct **Type of Word**.

> *What Type of Word MUST go in the blank?*
>
> *What is the Topic of the Sentence?*

15.   Don't _____ to fill out the
        questionnaire before you leave the
        meeting.

> *What Type of Word MUST go in the blank?*

16.   The car company is looking _____
        purchasing more raw materials from East
        Asia.

Sentences that allow more than one Type of Word to be correct

> *What Types of Words COULD go in the blank?*

17.   He is _____ helping us out today in
        the office.

> *Which Verb Tenses COULD go in the blank?*

18.   We still _____ to make greater profits
        next year due to increased trade with
        Europe.

Sentences that require more than one word in the Answer

> *What <u>Types</u> of Words MUST go in the blank?*

19.   We need to take another _____ the
        figures from last year's budget before we
        make any more cuts.

Answers on Page 85

> Context and grammar can sometimes make words that are usually uncountable into
> countable words. See www.englishclub.com/grammar/nouns-un-countable.htm

3. **Determine which Answer Choices don't fit with the sentence.**
   - For **Vocabulary Questions**: Ask yourself if Answer Choices fit the **Topic** of the Sentence.
   - For **Context Questions**: Ask yourself if Answer Choices fit the **Topic** of the Sentence.
   - For **Grammar Questions**: Ask yourself if Answer Choices fit the **Verb Tense** of the Sentence
   - For **Structure Questions**: Determine the **relationship** between the two parts of the sentence.

Using the Type of Word to eliminate Answer Choices

Which Answer Choices are more than one Type of Word? How are the meanings of those words different when they are different Types of Words?

20.   There will be a brief _____ after work
      to discuss next month's holiday agenda.

      (A) meeting
      (B) schedule
      (C) ceremony
      (D) meet

Using the Topic of the Sentence to eliminate Answer Choices

Which Answer Choices do not fit with the Topic of the Sentence? Why?

21.   We need more emergency supplies if we
      want to get through this _____.

      (A) celebration
      (B) crisis
      (C) cruise
      (D) conference

Using Context in the Sentence to determine correct Verb Tense of Answers

Which Answer Choices do not fit with the Verb Tenses of the Sentence? Why?

22.   We still _____ to make greater profits
      next year due to increased trade with
      Europe.

      (A) expecting
      (B) had expected
      (C) expect
      (D) have expected

Answers on Page 85

Determining the Relationship between two parts of a Sentence

What is the relationship between the first part of the sentence and the second part?

Which Answer Choices are wrong because they create the wrong relationship of ideas?

Which Answer Choices are wrong because they are grammatically incorrect?

23.   _____ the recent housing crisis, our home-building business is doing quite well.

(A) Because
(B) Because of
(C) Despite
(D) Even though

Answer on Page 85

Incomplete Sentence Tricks

Limited Fit
Opposite Meaning
Similar Meaning
Similar-Looking Word
Topic-Related /Wrong Topic
Wrong Form

Match the Trick to each Answer Choice below

Question: Everyone is happy they will receive a 5% _____ under the new contract.

____24. *employment*   (A) Limited Fit

____25. *raising*   (B) Opposite Meaning

____26. *elevation*   (C) Similar Meaning

____27. *cut*   (D) Similar-Looking Word

____28. *down*   (E) Topic-Related /Wrong Topic

____29. *praise*   (F) Wrong Form

Answers on Page 85

 If you can't choose between two Answer Choices, ASK: "What makes the meaning of each Answer Choice different from the others?"

The Incomplete Sentence Method Quiz

1. Compare _____ to identify the _____.

   Do most of the Answer Choices _____ but have _____?
       If "Yes" ➡ Vocabulary is being tested

   Do most of the Answer Choices _____ but have _____?
       If "Yes" ➡ Context is being tested

   Do all the Answer Choices have the _____?
       If "Yes" ➡ Grammar is being tested

   Do most the Answer Choices have _____, _____ or _____?
       If "Yes" ➡ Structure is being tested

   Some Questions may test more than one _____.

   Some Answer Choice words can be more than one _____..

2. Skim the sentence for _____.

   Determine the _____ of the Missing Word by skimming the sentence for _____.

   Skim the sentence to understand the _____.

   Remember that some Missing Words may be a combination of two different _____.

   Eliminate Answer Choices that are not the correct _____.

3. Determine which _____ don't fit with the _____.

   For **Vocabulary Questions**: Ask yourself if Answer Choices fit the _____ of the Sentence.

   For **Context Questions**: Ask yourself if Answer Choices fit the _____ of the Sentence.

   For **Grammar Questions**: Ask yourself if Answer Choices fit the _____ of the Sentence.

   For **Structure Questions**, determine the _____ between _____.

Answers on Page 73

Incomplete Sentence Quiz Exercises

Exercise 1: Type of Word of Answer Choices

Look at the Answer Choices and write down the Types of Words for each. If an Answer Choice could be more than one Type of Word, write down all of the possible types.

If the Answer Choice is a Verb, determine its Verb Tense.

Compare your answers with your partner and class.

Exercise 2: Type of Word of the blank + Topic of the Sentence

Look at the Sentence and determine what Type of Word could or must fit in the blank.

Look for Key Words to help you identify the Topic of the Sentence.

If the Answer Choices were Verbs, look for Key Words in the Sentence identifying the Verb Tenses in the Sentence.

Compare your answers with your partner and class.

Exercise 3: Answers & Tricks

Try to identify the correct Answer Choice.

Try to identify any Trick used by a wrong Answer Choice.

> *Limited Fit*
> *Opposite Meaning*
> *Similar Meaning*
> *Similar-Looking Words*
> *Topic-Related / Wrong Topic*
> *Wrong Form*

Compare your answers with your partner and class.

Answers to the Incomplete Sentence Quiz are on Page 85

101. The sales and marketing departments need to _____ their plans and activities to better serve the company's bottom line.

    (A) nominate
    (B) elevate
    (C) coordinate
    (D) designate

102. I thought the gift I had ordered would arrive before Christmas, but it's December 26th and it still hasn't _____ up.

    (A) show
    (B) showing
    (C) showed
    (D) shown

103. _____ people who enjoy their work need time to relax, it is hard to pull themselves away from their job.

    (A) Also
    (B) However
    (C) Even though
    (D) Despite

104. After the teachers found the school principal had given herself a 15% pay raise, they _____ plans to hold a strike.

    (A) formulate
    (B) formulated
    (C) formulating
    (D) formula

105. We thought that our online advertising campaign would be successful, but _____ has responded to the newsletter we sent out.

    (A) no one
    (B) anyone
    (C) someone
    (D) none

106. If you don't like the oven you bought, you can always return it for a full _____.

    (A) refund
    (B) charge
    (C) warranty
    (D) rebate

107. _____ the successful summer season, the manager doesn't think he can afford to add a new wing to the hotel.

    (A) Although
    (B) Because
    (C) Due to
    (D) Despite

108. Because of the snow storm, everyone at the airport _____ long departure delays to their flights.

    (A) anticipation
    (B) anticipating
    (C) anticipates
    (D) was anticipated

109. The new invoicing program _____ us to more quickly send out bills and process money last year.

    (A) allow
    (B) will allow
    (C) are allowing
    (D) allowed

110. Everyone expects the new pollution laws to pass and go into _____ at the end of this fiscal year.

    (A) affection
    (B) effective
    (C) affect
    (D) effect

111. Mrs. Regina's flight was postponed, enabling her to stay _____ Denver one more day.

   (A) on
   (B) to
   (C) until
   (D) in

112. The staff received _____ instructions not to open the conference room door until after the presentation.

   (A) explicit
   (B) explicitly
   (C) elicit
   (D) explication

113. It is very likely that because Mr. Wright cannot attend the meeting, _____ company will not receive the contract.

   (A) himself
   (B) his
   (C) he
   (D) him

114. In order to receive compensation for flood damage to your house, you need to _____ a claim with city hall.

   (A) file
   (B) purchase
   (C) ask for
   (D) receive

115. Sadly, the newspaper had to either cut its editorial staff _____ reduce pay for every employee working at the paper.

   (A) nor
   (B) but
   (C) and
   (D) or

116. We are within _____ of meeting our annual sales goals, thanks to our recent expansion into Asian markets.

   (A) length
   (B) sight
   (C) distance
   (D) seeing

117. In light of recent injuries, our workers need to be more _____ in how they stack boxes in the warehouse.

   (A) careless
   (B) care
   (C) carefully
   (D) careful

118. _____ recent developments in aviation technology, flight safety has increased dramatically for all airlines.

   (A) Resulting in
   (B) Because
   (C) Due to
   (D) Despite

119. The company CEO will be announcing new policies to all departments _____ the use of sick days.

   (A) regarding
   (B) among
   (C) to
   (D) from

120. Company profits _____ by 20% since we have installed the new high-speed computer network.

   (A) rise
   (B) risen
   (C) rising
   (D) have risen

121. If you purchase a car insurance policy with Allstate, you will receive a _____ oil change with Jiffy Lube.

    (A) complimentary
    (B) competitive
    (C) competing
    (D) complementary

122. Because of technical glitches, the R & D department is _____ schedule in releasing our newest generation of cell phones.

    (A) ahead
    (B) ahead of
    (C) behind
    (D) behind a

123. There are not many people who are able to quickly set up a computer network _____ inadvertently creating numerous software and hardware problems.

    (A) and also
    (B) with
    (C) without
    (D) when

124. Federal and state regulations state that only certified nurses are able to _____ medication to patients in hospitals.

    (A) administration
    (B) administrative
    (C) administering
    (D) administer

125. Mr. Garrison is best known for having started an international shipping company all on _____ at the age of 25.

    (A) his
    (B) his own
    (C) him
    (D) himself own

126. _____ recent news reports, it is very likely the central bank will raise interest rates next month.

    (A) According
    (B) According to
    (C) About to
    (D) Accounting for

127. Bay Area Transit provides _____ service to Tiburon every hour during weekdays.

    (A) routine
    (B) routines
    (C) routinely
    (D) route

128. In order to _____ its new line of young adult books, the publishers will conduct book-signings in various cities.

    (A) promotion
    (B) promoting
    (C) have promoted
    (D) promote

129. Albion Automotive _____ all of its cars are free of electronic defects for one year.

    (A) guarantee
    (B) guarantees
    (C) warranties
    (D) warranty

130. Five different contractors put in bids for the remodeling _____ at Sysco's headquarters.

    (A) guideline
    (B) project
    (C) policy
    (D) itinerary

131. The branch office _____ signs up the most new clients will be the recipient of the annual sales award.

    (A) who
    (B) where
    (C) which
    (D) when

132. The CEO sent a memo _____ that his company would be implementing new pollution controls during the next quarter.

    (A) states
    (B) statement
    (C) stated
    (D) stating

133. Mr. Isaak called to let the head office know that because of bad weather it was _____ that he would not be able to attend the meeting.

    (A) probable
    (B) probability
    (C) probably
    (D) problem

134. When Secretary Dillon left office, the oil company was left without a good _____ in the government's energy department.

    (A) compact
    (B) contact
    (C) connect
    (D) communication

135. _____ all of the brochures had been printed and sent to us, we paid the remaining balance to the printers.

    (A) Although
    (B) Except
    (C) Since
    (D) Despite

136. Mark Strong Elementary School welcomes all parents to donate _____ the annual fundraising campaign.

    (A) to
    (B) in
    (C) on
    (D) by

137. It took over 12 hours to get the union and company owners _____ on the terms of the new employee contracts.

    (A) agree
    (B) to agree
    (C) to agreeing
    (D) to agreed

138. _____ after receiving the phone call from his manager, Mr. Rogers ordered his staff to begin work on the new marketing campaign.

    (A) Immediately
    (B) Continually
    (C) Effectively
    (D) Reasonably

139. The interior designer gave us a rough _____ of the costs of bringing our house up to current safety standards.

    (A) escalate
    (B) increase
    (C) esteem
    (D) estimate

140. The courier had to be sent away because the package was not _____ ready to be delivered.

    (A) far
    (B) too
    (C) now
    (D) yet

Answers to the Incomplete Sentence Quiz are on Page 85

Incomplete Sentences Answers

(Method, pages 73-78)   *(Quiz, pages 81-84)*

Questions 1-14 answered in Class Discussions

9.	Grammar	101.	C	121.	A
10.	Context	102.	D	122.	C
11.	Structure	103.	C	123.	C
12.	Context	104.	B	124.	D
13.	Vocabulary & Grammar	105.	A	125.	B
14.	Grammar	106.	A	126.	B
15.	verb	107.	D	127.	A
16.	preposition	108.	C	128.	D
17.	adjective/adverb/verb	109.	D	129.	B
18.	many verb tenses	110.	D	130.	B
19.	noun + preposition	111.	D	131.	C
20.	A	112.	A	132.	D
21.	B	113.	B	133.	A
22.	C	114.	A	134.	B
23.	C	115.	D	135.	C
24.	E	116.	B	136.	A
25.	F	117.	D	137.	B
26.	C	118.	C	138.	A
27.	B	119.	A	139.	D
28.	A	120.	D	140.	D
29.	D				

MASTER
TEXT COMPLETION

Directions for this Part of the TOEIC: Read the texts that follow. A word or phrase is missing in some of the sentences. Four Answer Choices are given for each of the sentences. Select the best answer to complete the text. Then mark the letter (A), (B), (C), or (D) on your answer sheet.

The Text Completion Method

1. **Skim the Text to determine its Topic and Main Ideas.**

   - Look at **Headings** at the top of the page and **Titles** in the Text Box.
   - Skim the Text for **Purpose Words**, **Action Verbs**, **Adjectives**, and **Main Nouns**.

2. **Compare the Answer Choices to identify the Type of Question.**

   - Do most Answer Choices *look similar* but have *different meanings*?   ➡ **Vocabulary** is being tested
   - Do most Answer Choices *look different* but have *similar meanings*?   ➡ **Context** is being tested
   - Do most Answer Choices have the *same root word*?   ➡ **Grammar** is being tested
   - Do most Answer Choices have *conjunctions, participles or prepositions*? ➡ **Structure** is being tested
   - Some Questions may be a mix of two different Types of Questions.

3. **Look for Clues before and after the Missing Word.**

   - Look before and after the Missing Word for **Grammar and Context Clues**.
   - Remember that some Missing Words may be a combination of **two different Types of Words**.
   - Eliminate Answer Choices that are not the correct **Type of Word**.

4. **Determine which Answer Choices don't fit with the sentence.**

   - For **Vocabulary Questions**: Ask yourself if Answer Choices fit the **Topic** of the Sentence.
   - For **Context Questions**: Ask yourself if Answer Choices fit the **Topic** of the Sentence.
   - For **Grammar Questions**: Ask yourself if Answer Choices fit the **Verb Tense** of the Sentence.
   - For **Structure Questions**: Determine the **relationship** between the two parts of the sentence.

1. Skim the Text to determine its Topic and Main Ideas.
- Look at **Headings** at the top of the page and **Titles** in the Text Box.
- Skim the Text for **Purpose Words**, **Action Verbs**, **Adjectives**, and **Main Nouns**.

The most common Types of Texts

advertisements	*faxes*	*memos*	*news articles*
notices	*emails*	*letters*	

Skimming the Text

Focus on words that give you an understanding of the **Topic**, **Purpose**, **General Information**, or **Main Ideas**.

- **Subject** or **Object** of each sentence
- **Action Verbs** or **Phrasal Verbs**
- **Helping Verbs**
- **Strong Adjectives**

- **Who** is doing **something** (or *requesting* something)
- **Why, when or where something is happening**
- **How** something is happening

Skim the Text below and <u>underline</u> Key Words that help you understand its meaning

---

Questions 141 through 144 refer to the following email.

From: f.allerton@microsoft.com
To: j.rommel@apple.com
Re: Friday Meeting
Date: 12/1/11

Dear Mr. Rommel,

I am writing to get some _____ details regarding your trip to Seattle for the financial meeting this Friday. We will have a company car at the airport to _____ and take you to your hotel, but we need to know at what time your flight _____, along with your flight number. A representative will wait for you at baggage claim—he will be holding a _____ with your name and our company logo.

Sincerely,

Francis

What Type of Text is this?

What is the Topic of the Text?

What Key Words tell you the purpose of the Text?

See next page for a sample skim of this text

*(Key Words are in **BOLD**)*

From: f.allerton@microsoft.com
To: j.rommel@apple.com
Re: Friday Meeting
Date: 12/1/11

Dear **Mr. Rommel,**

I am **writing to get** some _____ **details** regarding **your trip** to **Seattle** for the financial **meeting** this **Friday.** We will have a company **car at** the **airport** to _____ and **take you** to your **hotel,** but we **need to know** at what **time** your **flight** _____, along with your **flight number.** A **representative** will **wait for you** at **baggage claim**—he will be **holding a** _____ with **your name** and our **company logo.**

Sincerely,

Francis

Skim the Text below and <u>underline</u> Key Words that help you understand its meaning.

Questions 145 through 148 refer to the following advertisement.

> **Hawaiian Tropics Vacations Summer Sale!**
>
> Are you ready to enjoy the warm summer sun in the most beautiful place in the world? Then _____ our website and see the amazing deals we have for you! Find the best travel deals and cheap airline tickets to help you plan your next _____ trip. Don't forget to complement your inexpensive airfares by _____ advantage of our great prices on hotel and car rentals! Our expert travel agents are _____ to helping you with your next trip to Hawaii, getting you the best deals possible.

What Type of Text is this?

What is the Topic of the Text?

What Key Words tell you the purpose of the Text?

You only want to spend about 30 seconds skimming the Text to get a general idea of its Topic, Purpose and Main Ideas.

2. Compare the Answer Choices to identify the Type of Question.

- Do most Answer Choices *look similar* but have *different meanings*?   ➡ **Vocabulary** is being tested
- Do most Answer Choices *look different* but have *similar meanings*?   ➡ **Context** is being tested
- Do most Answer Choices have the *same root word*?   ➡ **Grammar** is being tested
- Do most Answer Choices have *conjunctions, participles or prepositions*? ➡ **Structure** is being tested
- Some Questions may be a mix of two different Types of Questions.

Vocabulary Questions

What Types of Words are these?

1.
(A) minimize
(B) immunity
(C) enmity
(D) community

2.
(A) regulation
(B) regular
(C) regime
(D) regimented

Context Questions

What Types of Words are these?

Which Answer Choices have <u>similar</u> meanings? How are they different?

Which Answer Choices have <u>opposite</u> meanings?

3.
(A) go over
(B) explore
(C) examination
(D) discover

4.
(A) affect
(B) effect
(C) consequence
(D) change

Grammar Questions

What Types of Words are these?

5.
(A) propose
(B) proposal
(C) proposition
(D) prompt

6.
(A) withheld
(B) withhold
(C) withdrawn
(D) with holding

Structure Questions

What Types of Words are these?

Which Answer Choices have <u>similar</u> meanings? How are they different?

Which Answer Choices have <u>opposite</u> meanings?

7. (A) toward
    (B) at
    (C) away from
    (D) closely

8. (A) passed by
    (B) met
    (C) seen
    (D) engaged

9. (A) although
    (B) though
    (C) since
    (D) despite

10. (A) effect
    (B) effectively
    (C) necessary
    (D) essential

Identify the Types of Question for each set of Answer Choices below

11. (A) increase
    (B) decrease
    (C) enlarge
    (D) shrink

12. (A) look out
    (B) looked in
    (C) looking over
    (D) looked at

13. (A) mediate
    (B) mediation
    (C) meditate
    (D) immediately

14. (A) Also
    (B) However
    (C) Despite
    (D) How

15. (A) farther
    (B) further
    (C) near
    (D) closer

16. (A) carefully
    (B) cared
    (C) cairn
    (D) carcinogen

17. (A) and
    (B) but
    (C) excluding
    (D) plus

18. (A) himself
    (B) myself
    (C) itself
    (D) my

19. (A) at
    (B) on
    (C) over
    (D) in

20. (A) refund
    (B) rebate
    (C) warranty
    (D) reward

3. Look for Clues before and after the Missing Word.

- Look before and after the Missing Word for **Grammar and Context Clues**.
- Remember that some Missing Words may be a combination of **two different Types of Words**.
- Eliminate Answer Choices that are not the correct **Type of Word**.

Grammar & Context Clues

Look at the sentences below and answer the following questions for each sentence.

> *What words identify the topic of the sentence?*
>
> *What Types of Words could or must go in the blank?*
>
> *What words help you identify the Type of Word needed for the Answer?*

21.   We are looking for volunteers to help us distribute fliers in the local _____.

22.   We need to take a second look _____ the figures from last year's budget before we make any more cuts.

23.   Have you _____ the newest model of the Audi sports car?

24.   The human resource _____ feels that we need to change the medical insurance plans we offer our employees.

Sentences that require more than one word in the Answer

> *What <u>Types</u> of Words MUST go in the blank?*

25.   I had to _____ the new coffee maker because it had a defective filter.

26.   Do you know anyone who knows _____ turn off the fire alarm?

Answers on Page 100

4. Determine which Answer Choices don't fit with the sentence.

- For **Vocabulary Questions**: Ask yourself if Answer Choices fit the **Topic** of the Sentence.
- For **Context Questions**: Ask yourself if Answer Choices fit the **Topic** of the Sentence.
- For **Grammar Questions**: Ask yourself if Answer Choices fit the **Verb Tense** of the Sentence
- For **Structure Questions**: Determine the **relationship** between the two parts of the sentence.

Using the Type of Word to eliminate Answer Choices

Which Answer Choices are more than one Type of Word?

How are the meanings of those words different when they are different Types of Words?

27.   We need to meet this week to decide how our new _____ campaign will roll out.

     (A) markets
     (B) market
     (C) marketed
     (D) marketing

Using the Topic of the Sentence to eliminate Answer Choices

Which Answer Choices do not fit with the Topic of the Sentence? Why?

28.   Car prices fell by an average of 5 percent last week due to a _____ in the cost of steel.

     (A) drop
     (B) rise
     (C) leveling
     (D) guarantee

Using Context in the Sentence to determine correct Verb Tense of Answers

Which Answer Choices do not fit with the Verb Tenses of the Sentence? Why?

29.   The company CEO doesn't know that his office _____ remodeled next week.

     (A) has been
     (B) is going to be
     (C) was going to be
     (D) is

Answers on Page 100

Determining the Relationship between two parts of a Sentence

What is the relationship between the first part of the sentence and the second part?

Which Answer Choices are wrong because they create the wrong relationship of ideas?

Which Answer Choices are wrong because they are grammatically incorrect?

30.   _____, because my car broke down
       this morning, I will not be able to take you
       to the airport.

       (A) Unfortunately
       (B) Consequently
       (C) Admittedly
       (D) Luckily

The importance of Idioms

Which Answer Choices are grammatically possible?

Which Answer Choices fit the context of the sentence?

Which Answer Choices create an idiom you have heard before?

31.   I am _____ I cannot help you with this
       project, because it is outside my area of
       expertise.

       (A) happy
       (B) enjoying
       (C) afraid
       (D) unable

32.   It was definitely a pleasure to _____
       you at the annual conference.

       (A) talk
       (B) discuss with
       (C) show
       (D) meet

Answers on Page 100

A majority of questions test your knowledge of common Business Idioms. Study Business English Idioms!

Choosing between two Answer Choices

Always be asking: *"What makes the meaning of each Answer Choice different from the others?"*

> ***Which Answer Choices have similar meanings?***
>
> ***What makes the meaning of each Answer Choice different from the others?***

33.   We need to _____ the numbers from
        last year's budget one more time before
        we can make any decisions.

        (A) go over
        (B) explore
        (C) examination
        (D) discover

Answer on Page 100

Text Completion Tricks

Similar-Looking Word
Similar Meaning
Topic-Related /Wrong Topic
Wrong Form
Opposite Meaning

> ***Match the Trick to each Answer Choice below***

Question: The deadline for _____ for the in-house 'Innovations in Marketing' contest has been
                  pushed back to March 22nd.

_____34. applications   (A) Similar-Looking Word

_____35. marketers   (B) Opposite Meaning

_____36. submits   (C) Similar Meaning

_____37. subjecting   (D) Topic-Related / Wrong Topic

_____38. withdrawals   (E) Wrong Form

Answers on Page 100

Answers from one part of the Text may help you with answers in other parts of the Text—use
them as new clues to help you.

The Text Completion Method Quiz

1. **Skim the Text** to determine its _____ and _____.

    Look at _____ at the top of the page and _____ in the Text Box.

    Skim the Text for _____, _____, _____, and _____.

2. **Compare** the Answer Choices to identify the _____.

    Vocabulary Questions: Do most of the Answer Choices _____ but have _____?

    Context Questions Do most of the Answer Choices _____ but have _____?

    Grammar Questions Do all the Answer Choices have the _____?

    Structure Questions Do most the Answer Choices have _____, _____ or _____?

    Some Questions may be a mix of two different _____.

3. **Look for** _____ before and after the _____.

    Look before and after the Missing Word for _____ and _____ Clues.

    Some Missing Words may be a combination of two different _____.

3. Determine which _____ don't fit with the _____.

    For **All Questions**: Eliminate Answer Choices that are not the correct _____.

    For **Vocabulary Questions**: Ask yourself if Answer Choices fit the _____ of the Sentence.

    For **Context Questions**: Ask yourself if Answer Choices fit the _____ of the Sentence.

    For **Grammar Questions**: Ask yourself if Answer Choices fit the _____ of the Sentence.

    For **Structure Questions**, determine the _____ between _____.

Answers on Page 86

Text Completion Quiz Exercises

Exercise 1: Skimming

Skim the Text for Key Words in the **Headings** and **Titles**.

Skim the Text and find **Purpose Words**, **Action Verbs**, **Adjectives**, and **Main Nouns**. Try to group them together to create meaning.

Compare your answers with your partner and class.

Exercise 2: Question Type, Part of Speech, and Related Meanings

Look at the Answer Choices and try to identify the **Type of each Question** and the **Type of Word that could or must go in the blank**.

See if there are Answer Choices that are **Similar Meaning** or **Opposite Meaning** to each other, and which Answer Choices are the **wrong Type of Word**.

Compare your answers with your partner and class.

Exercise 3: Answers & Tricks

Try to identify the correct Answer Choice.

Try to identify any Trick used by a wrong Answer Choice.

> *Opposite Meaning*
> *Similar Meaning*
> *Similar-Looking Words*
> *Topic-Related / Wrong Topic*
> *Wrong Form*

Compare your answers with your partner and class.

Answers to the Text Completion Quiz are on Page 100

Questions 141 through 144 refer to the following memo.

Date: October 16
To: All Employees
From: Janice Lee, Recycling Coordinator
RE: Recycling Program

I wanted to let you all know that currently we are doing a pretty good job recycling. However, we could be doing better. Not only is it important that we do our ------- to help the community we work and live

141. (A) sharing
(B) share
(C) shared
(D) shares

in; recycling has an ------- benefit of reducing our company's waste disposal expenses, which

142. (A) more
(B) adding
(C) increasing
(D) additional

helps improve our bottom line. And, of course, recycling helps preserve natural resources – every ton of paper recycled saves 17 trees!

With this in mind, I would like to ------- everyone of the recycling opportunities available. The

143. (A) remember
(B) remind
(C) memory
(D) memorize

attached flyer describes what we can recycle. I encourage you to read this information carefully and actively participate in the program. In addition, if you wish to ------- a recycling container for your

144. (A) give
(B) abstain
(C) obtain
(D) object

work area, just call me.

Questions 145 through 148 refer to the following fax.

To: All Icebreakers customers
From: Rhonda Xerxes, Icebreakers Customer Service Director
Fax: 341-987-0987
Subject: New Service Call Policy
Date: 2/2/2009

Because more customers are paying their monthly fees later and later, we are ------- to set down a

145. (A) force
(B) forceful
(C) forcing
(D) forced

new company policy regarding service calls. If a customer is more than 15 days late in their monthly payment and their ice machine is not working, customers will still be able to contact us to fix the machine; however, we will expect payment in full of any unpaid ------- due at the time of our visit.

146. (A) balance
(B) revenue
(C) income
(D) profit

While I am sorry that we must go to such extremes as those outlined above, I am ------- that there is no

147. (A) afraid
(B) fearful
(C) happy
(D) feared

alternative. This new policy will go ------- effect March 30, 2009. If there are any questions regarding

148. (A) to
(B) for
(C) into
(D) from

our new policy, please give me a call.

Questions 149 through 152 refer to the following letter.

Ms. Margaret Hampton
Michigan Gas & Electric
670 SW 1st Avenue
Detroit, MI 80453

Dear Ms. Hampton,

I am excited to apply for the position of executive secretary that you advertised Sunday in the
Detroit Independent ------- week. As the head secretary at Renfield Real Estate, I answered to

149. (A) previous
(B) last
(C) next
(D) former

Mr. Ron Paul, the company's owner. While my normal duties were the ------- typing, and filing, I

150. (A) unusual
(B) using
(C) usually
(D) usual

was also responsible for scheduling all of Mr. Paul's appointments, screening his telephone calls and visitors,
and organizing his paperwork and correspondence. From working at Renfield Real Estate, I have become
------- with the duties of an executive secretary and believe I can anticipate and meet the expectations

151. (A) learning
(B) known
(C) familiarity
(D) familiar

you have for a secretary. I would love the opportunity to discuss my qualifications with you in
person.------- I am busy each morning, I am available to meet any day in the afternoon.

152. (A) Even though
(B) However
(C) So
(D) Despite

Warm regards,

Olga Pastrova

Answers to the Text Completion Quiz are on Page 100

Text Completion Answers

(Method, pages 86-94)   *(Quiz, pages 97-99)*

Questions 1-10 answered in Class Discussions

11.	Context	141. B
12.	Grammar & Structure	142. D
13.	Vocabulary & Grammar	143. B
14.	Structure	144. C
15.	Context	145. D
16.	Vocabulary & Grammar	146. A
17.	Structure	147. A
18.	Context	148. C
19.	Structure	149. B
20.	Context	150. D
21.	noun	151. D
22.	preposition	152. A
23.	verb	
24.	noun	
25.	verb	
26.	adverb + preposition	
27.	D	
28.	A	
29.	B	
30.	A	
31.	C	
32.	D	
33.	A	
34.	C	
35.	D	
36.	E	
37.	A	
38.	B	

MASTER
READING COMPREHENSION

The Reading Comprehension Method

1. **Skim Headings and Titles.**

   - Use Headings and Titles to determine **Text Structure** and **Topic**.
   - **For Double Texts**: Identify the **Relationship** between the two Texts.

2. **Determine the Type of each Question.**

   - Decide which Questions you will answer first.
   - Beware of "**NOT**" Questions—these have 3 "Correct" Answers and 1 "Wrong" Answer.

3. **Answer Detail Questions.**

   - Find **ALL** locations in the Text where **Key Words** of an Answer Choice and Question are mentioned.

4. **Answer Topic/Main Idea Questions.**

   - Focus on finding Action Verbs in the **first 1-2 sentences** and **last 1-2 sentences** of the Text.

5. **Answer Purpose Questions.**

   - Scan for **Action Verbs** from the Answer Choices.

6. **Answer Inference Questions.**

   - Find **ALL** locations in the Text where **Key Words** of an Answer Choice and Question are mentioned.

1. Skim Headings and Titles.

- Use Headings and Titles to determine **Text Structure** and **Topic**.
- **For Double Texts**: Identify the **Relationship** between the two Texts.

Circle Key Words in the Headings and Titles of each Text

Text 1

What kind of company is Walden?

Questions 153 and 155 refer to the following table.

Shipping Rate for Walden Company

Domestic Standard		International Standard
Boots	$3.99	$12.49
Sandals	$2.98	$6.89
Runners	$2.98	$12.29

Text 2

What does "Re:" mean?

Questions 173 through 176 refer to the following memo.

Memo
To: All sales staff From: Randal Smith, Head of Sales & Marketing Re: Future sales meetings Date: June 2nd Last week I talked with our boss, and she agreed…

Text 3

Who sent this letter? What company does he work for?

Who received this letter? What company does he work for?

Questions 191 through 195 refer to the following letter and invoice.

> Customer Service Dept.
> RSL Rentals
> 4526 SE Stark
> Portland, OR 98344
>
> October 2, 2008
>
> REF: #1047
> Sacred Hills Wedding Chapel
> 12344 SE Wanda Drive
> Portland, OR 98354
>
> Dear Mr. Iglesias,
>
> I am writing in reference to…look forward to your prompt reply.
>
> Sincerely,
>
> Jon Weyr
> Head Service Director

Double Texts

Common relationships between Double Texts:

- Text #2 *answers a question* asked in Text #1
- Text #2 *explains information* in Text #1 (or the reverse, Text #1 explaining Text #2)
- Text #2 *gives information* that was *requested* in Text #1

Underline words in each Text that help you understand their relationship to each other

---

Hi Margaret,

Thank you for sending in your resume for the open position at RS Commerce & Exchange. After going over your resume and other documents, I believe that you are more than qualified for the position of financial department head. We were particularly impressed with the numerous recommendations from both supervisors and clients you submitted with your resume.

Because we are looking to fill this position as soon as possible, I would like to schedule an interview with you next week. This interview would include Jeffrey Saks, our CEO, Rina Todd, our HR manager, and me. I could also give you a brief tour of our company facilities at that time. Because I will be out of town from Monday to Wednesday, I would be available Thursday or Friday morning.

John

Hi John,

Thank you for contacting me about the position at your company. I would very much like to come and see you sometime next week, but I am currently out of town and will not be back until the week after next. I could come in for an interview either Thursday or Friday of that week. I would be free to meet you at any time on either of those days; please let me know what works best for you and I will be there. Thank you, and I look forward to meeting you and your colleague then.

Margaret

Tables are often easier to understand than other types of texts. Focus on answering questions connected to Tables and Charts.

2. Determine the Type of each Question.

- Decide which Questions you will answer first.
- Beware of "**NOT**" Questions—these have 3 "Correct" Answers and 1 "Wrong" Answer.

Which of these Questions do you think would be easier to answer? Why?

Underline Key Words in the Questions and Answer Choices

1. How long was last year's marketing conference?

   (A) Less than 24 hours
   (B) 1 day
   (C) 2 days
   (D) Over 3 days

2. According to the memo, why does Williams only moderate one discussion?

   (A) He needs to finish his annual report that evening
   (B) He needs to go home after lunch that day and take care of his children
   (C) He is volunteering for a local charity
   (D) He wanted to give his two afternoon discussion assignments to Gregory

3. Which of the following is most likely true?

   (A) Phyllis wants to cancel her order
   (B) Phyllis did not specify when she wanted the delivery
   (C) Michael forgot to subtract the amount Phyllis prepaid
   (D) Michael didn't add the delivery fee to the invoice

NOT & EXCEPT Questions

What is different about these questions? What are they asking you to do?

4. What is Lyle NOT requesting?

5. Verna is concerned about all the following issues EXCEPT

6. What is Albert not asking about?

Unlike other NOT Questions, Questions with a lower-case "not" are usually asking for something directly stated in the Text.

3. Answer Detail Questions.

- Find **ALL** locations in the Text where **Key Words** of an Answer Choice and Question are mentioned.

What are common types of Detail Questions?

- *Skim the Questions and Answer Choices for Key Words*

- *Scan the Text to find Question Key Words*

- *Skim before and after the Question Key Words in the Text*

- *Look for Answer Choice Key Words nearby the Question Key Words*

You are ready to enjoy the warm summer sun in the most beautiful place in the world. You deserve to spend your vacation swimming among turtles and walking along a warm tropical beach without a care in the world. You want to visit Hawaii, but don't feel you can afford the trip?

You can!

HonoluluHighlights.com is *the* best place to go to live your tropical dreams. Visit our website and see the amazing deals we have for you! Find the best travel deals and cheap airline tickets to help you plan your next trip to the Hawaiian Isles. Whether you plan on a visit to historic Oahu, hike through Kawai, or surf the waves of Maui, we are here to help. Don't forget to complement our inexpensive airfares by also taking advantage of our great prices on hotel and car rentals! We also offer discounts on special shows and outdoor excursions on every major Hawaiian island.

---

7.   What can you find at this website?

   (A) Information on Hawaiian history
   (B) Discount airline tickets
   (C) A list of the best Hawaiian beaches
   (D) Maps of hiking trails

8.   What does this website NOT offer?

   (A) Flights tickets
   (B) Discounts on car rentals
   (C) Cheap prices on hotels
   (D) Cruise ship tickets

Answers on Page 129

Some Inference Questions look like Detail Questions. If it is hard to answer a Detail Question, it might actually be an Inference Question.

4. Answer Topic/Main Idea Questions.

• Focus on finding Action Verbs in the **first 1-2 sentences** and **last 1-2 sentences** of the Text.

What is a Topic Question?

• *Skim the Questions and Answer Choices for Key Words*

• *Look at Titles and Headings of the Text*

• *Scan the 1st & 2nd sentence in the Text, looking for Key Words from the Answer Choices*

• *If the topic/main idea is not clear in the 1st & 2nd sentences, Scan the last 1 or 2 sentences*

You are ready to enjoy the warm summer sun in the most beautiful place in the world. You deserve to spend your vacation swimming among turtles and walking along a warm tropical beach without a care in the world. You want to visit Hawaii, but don't feel you can afford the trip?

You can!

HonoluluHighlights.com is *the* best place to go to live your tropical dreams. Visit our website and see the amazing deals we have for you! Find the best travel deals and cheap airline tickets to help you plan your next trip to the Hawaiian Isles. Whether you plan on a visit to historic Oahu, hike through Kawai, or surf the waves of Maui, we are here to help. Don't forget to complement our inexpensive airfares by also taking advantage of our great prices on hotel and car rentals! We also offer discounts on special shows and outdoor excursions on every major Hawaiian island.

---

9.   What is this advertisement trying to sell?

(A) Beautiful tropical beaches
(B) Jobs at a travel agency
(C) Affordable tickets for flights to Hawaii
(D) Discounted houses for sale on Hawaii

Answer on Page 129

If the Text is an Advertisement, the Topic or Purpose of the Text may be in the middle of the Text.

5. Answer Purpose Questions.

• Scan for **Action Verbs** from the Answer Choices.

What is a Purpose Question?

• *Skim the Questions and Answer Choices for Key Words*

• *Scan the Text to find Question Key Words*

• *Skim before and after the Question Key Words in the Text*

• *Look for Answer Choice Key Words nearby the Question Key Words, especially Action Verbs*

• *Look for Conjunctions such as "because", "for", "so", "in order to", or "as"*

You are ready to enjoy the warm summer sun in the most beautiful place in the world. You deserve to spend your vacation swimming among turtles and walking along a warm tropical beach without a care in the world. You want to visit Hawaii, but don't feel you can afford the trip?

You can!

HonoluluHighlights.com is *the* best place to go to live your tropical dreams. Visit our website and see the amazing deals we have for you! Find the best travel deals and cheap airline tickets to help you plan your next trip to the Hawaiian Isles. Whether you plan on a visit to historic Oahu, hike through Kawai, or surf the waves of Maui, we are here to help. Don't forget to complement our inexpensive airfares by also taking advantage of our great prices on hotel and car rentals! We also offer discounts on special shows and outdoor excursions on every major Hawaiian island.

---

10.   Why does the ad recommend visiting the website?

   (A) To learn why Hawaii is famous
   (B) To learn more about the website's offers
   (C) To discover where you can swim with turtles
   (D) To learn how to set up a travel discount website

Answer on Page 129

The TOEIC often hide correct answers by using synonyms of key words. If you can't find the answer, you probably missed a synonym.

6. Answer Inference Questions.

• Find **ALL** locations in the Text where **Key Words** of an Answer Choice and Question are mentioned.

What words help you identify Inference Questions?

• *Skim the Questions and Answer Choices for Key Words*

• *Scan the Text to find ALL locations of Question Key Words*

• *Skim before and after the Question Key Words in the Text*

• *Look for Answer Choice Key Words nearby the Question Key Words*

You are ready to enjoy the warm summer sun in the most beautiful place in the world. You deserve to spend your vacation swimming among turtles and walking along a warm tropical beach without a care in the world. You want to visit Hawaii, but don't feel you can afford the trip?

You can!

HonoluluHighlights.com is *the* best place to go to live your tropical dreams. Visit our website and see the amazing deals we have for you! Find the best travel deals and cheap airline tickets to help you plan your next trip to the Hawaiian Isles. Whether you plan on a visit to historic Oahu, hike through Kawai, or surf the waves of Maui, we are here to help. Don't forget to complement our inexpensive airfares by also taking advantage of our great prices on hotel and car rentals! We also offer discounts on special shows and outdoor excursions on every major Hawaiian island.

---

11.   Who is probably not interested in this
        advertisement?

        (A) Someone who wants to go on a
            vacation
        (B) Someone not living in Hawaii
        (C) Someone who enjoys the outdoors
        (D) Someone who does not like to fly

Answer on Page 129

It is easier to determine wrong answers to Inference Questions than prove correct
Answers. Focus on proving answers wrong.

Reading Comprehension Tricks

Extreme Inference
Incorrect Paraphrase
Similar Type of Detail
Topic-Related /Wrong Topic
Wrong Detail

Hi Margaret,

Thank you for sending in your resume for the open position at RS Commerce & Exchange. After going over your resume and other documents, I believe that you are more than qualified for the position of financial department head. We were particularly impressed with the numerous recommendations from both supervisors and clients you submitted with your resume.

Because we are looking to fill this position as soon as possible, I would like to schedule an interview with you next week. This interview would include Jeffrey Saks, our CEO, Rina Todd, our HR manager, and me. I could also give you a brief tour of our company facilities at that time. Because I will be out of town from Monday to Wednesday, I would be available Thursday or Friday morning.

John

Create wrong answers for the Questions below.

Compare your Answer Choices with a partner.

Can you identify the Trick your partner used for each of their Answer Choices?

---

12.   What is the purpose of this email?"

(A) _____

(B) _____

(C) _____

13.   When is John available to meet Margaret?

(A) _____

(B) _____

(C) _____

14.   According to the email, why did John think Margaret's resume was exceptional?"

(A) _____

(B) _____

(C) _____

If you can't choose between two Answer Choices, ASK: "What makes the meaning of each Answer Choice different from the others?"

The Reading Comprehension Method Quiz

1. **Skim** _____ **and** _____.

   Use _____ and _____ to determine _____ and _____.

   For Double Texts: Identify the _____ between the two Texts.

2. **Determine the** _____.

   Beware of _____ Questions—these have 3 _____ Answers and 1 _____ Answer.

3. **Answer** _____ **Questions.**

   Find _____ locations in the Text where Key Words of an _____ and _____ are mentioned.

4. **Answer** _____ **Questions.**

   Focus on finding _____ in the _____ and _____ of the Text.

5. **Answer** _____ **Questions.**

   Scan for _____ from the Answer Choices.

6. **Answer** _____ **Questions.**

   Find _____ in the Text where _____ of an Answer Choice and Question are mentioned.

Answers on Page 101

Reading Comprehension Quiz Exercises

Exercise 1: Purpose of the Text

Skim each Text and circle the words that tell you the following:

Heading
Titles
Purpose given at beginning of Text
Purpose given at end of Text

For Double Text Questions, determine **how and why the two Texts are connected to each other.**

Exercise 2: Question & Answer Choice Key Words

Circle the Key Words in each Question and Answer Choice.

Example:

Which flight is she taking?

(A)   The one to San Francisco
(B)   The midnight flight
(C)   The first flight tomorrow morning
(D)   The one to Seattle

For each Text, decide which Questions look easiest to do. Answer those Questions first.

Exercise 3: Answers & Tricks

Try to identify the correct Answer Choice.

Try to identify any Trick used by a wrong Answer Choice.

Extreme Inference
Incorrect Paraphrase
Similar Type of Detail
Topic-Related / Wrong Topic
Wrong Detail

Compare your answers with your partner and class.

Answers to the Reading Comprehension Quiz are on Page 129

Questions 153 and 155 refer to the following table.

Shipping Rates for Walden Books						
Domestic Standard*		**Domestic Expedited#**	**Two Day**	**Overnight**	**International Standard***	**International Expedited#**
Books	$3.99	$6.99	$11.98	$17.98	$12.49	$35.98
CDs, Cassettes	$2.98	$5.19	$7.98	$11.98	$6.89	$32.98
VHS Videotapes	$2.98	$5.19	$11.98	$17.98	$12.29	$35.98
DVDs	$2.98	$5.19	$7.98	$11.98	$12.29	$32.98

*Standard: Domestic (U.S. & Canada): 9-12 Business Days / International: 13-18 Business days
 # Expedited: Domestic: 3-5 Business Days / International 6-8 Business days

NOTE: All prices above are for packages weighing less than 20 lbs. For packages weighing 20 lbs. or more, all shipping rates are doubled.

Two Day & Overnight service is only available for shipments to locations in the U.S. & Canada.

153.   Where might you expect to see this table?

(A) A travel book
(B) A video store
(C) A website
(D) An instructional manual

154.   How are shipping times for standard packages estimated?

(A) By cost
(B) By destination
(C) By type of item shipped
(D) By weight

155.   How much would it cost to ship a 30 lbs. package of books to California overnight?

(A) $11.98
(B) $17.98
(C) $35.96
(D) $35.98

Questions 156 through 158 refer to the following advertisement.

Are you paying too much calling overseas?

Do you feel that with the money you spent calling a friend or loved one in another country you could have flown to see them?

Don't let that happen to you!

Save 50% on your next international phone call when you switch to CONNEXUS, the leading international telecommunication company in over 30 countries. Simply call 1-800-CONNEXUS, and tell us which country you call the most—and lock in a 50% discount for all calls to that country for the next year!* We will even help you in switching from your current international call carrier to us by contacting your current carrier and doing all the work for you! It's never been more easy or rewarding to join CONNEXUS!

We understand that with family and friends all over the world, you need an inexpensive and reliable service to help you keep in touch with those you love--CONNEXUS, with over 10 years experience and one of the most advanced networks on the planet, is there for you.

*Based on comparisons of the top 5 international call carrier companies. See www.connexus.com for more details on how to lock in our 50% "Favorite Country" rate! Call a customer service representative today!

---

156.   What is purpose of this advertisement?

        (A) To encourage calls overseas
        (B) To encourage people to change their overseas call carrier
        (C) To promote a new international telecommunication company
        (D) To ask how much money people spend calling overseas

157.   How many countries does CONNEXUS operate in?

        (A) 5
        (B) 30
        (C) Half of all countries
        (D) Over 30

158.   According to the ad, what can you do to switch to CONNEXUS?

        (A) Call your current carrier
        (B) Call CONNEXUS
        (C) Visit the CONNEXUS website
        (D) Pick 30 favorite countries

Questions 159 through 161 refer to the following news release.

NEWS RELEASE

City Club of Akron
Arkon, Ohio 75243
Yasmine Ulrich, Publicity Director
Fax: (804) 771-1222

Alice Wrigley, Editor
Akron Sentinel
Fax: (804) 757-4534

FOR IMMEDIATE RELEASE

Akron, Ohio, September 10, 2009. Herbert Walker, former president and CEO of Medco Digital, Inc., was named "Citizen of the Year" at the annual City Club of Akron Honors Night on September 9. During his two years since leaving Medco Digital, Mr. Walker has been involved in dozens of philanthropic endeavors throughout the region, with a majority of those activities centered in Akron itself.

In accepting the award, Mr. Walker announced the kick-off of a new fundraising drive for the Akron Economic Opportunities Movement (AEON), dedicated to reducing the number of homeless living downtown. To help the drive for donations, Mr. Walker promised that he would match every individual donation of $500 or more, declaring that, "It is up to us, the fortunate members of the Akron community, to help lift up those among us less fortunate."

At the awards ceremony, Mr. Walker, aged 67, stated his never-ending desire to work on behalf of others, mainly due to his desire to help other achieve economic security and prosperity. He explained that, "My hometown has given me so much over the years," and that he has been "blessed with opportunities and aid which have helped [me] achieve many things in business."

A native of Akron, Mr. Walker created Medco Digital in 1974, building it up to be a national leader in the electronic medical equipment industry. He has been a longtime supporter of many local charities and non-profit organizations, helping out through personal donations, volunteering and fundraising campaigns. The list of his humanitarian activities was so long that according to Philip Regence, Akron City Club President, "It would have taken over 10 minutes to list all the things Herbert has done for our city and the state."

---

159. What is the main purpose of this letter?

(A) To explain why Mr. Walker is a philanthropist
(B) To raise money for AEON
(C) To announce an award given to Mr. Walker
(D) To ask for support from local charities

160. Who will probably be helped by the new AEON fundraising campaign?

(A) Anyone donating $500 to AEON
(B) A member of the Akron City Club
(C) Someone needing support with a mortgage
(D) Someone who lives on the street

161. What kind of company is Medco Digital?

(A) An electronic device company
(B) A fundraising organization
(C) A marketing company
(D) A hospital

Questions 162 through 164 refer to the following notice.

Notice to Passengers

Pacific Airways would like to inform passengers of a change in our baggage check-in policy—this policy takes effect March 1, 2010.

As of March 1, 2010, for bags weighing more than 40 lbs, a $50 over-weight fee will be added to the normal $20 check-in luggage fee.

This change in check-in policy is to aid Pacific Airways in speeding-up the loading and unloading of baggage onto airplanes. Studies conducted by several independent system analysis companies have found that large, heavy bags slow down the loading and unloading of airplanes, resulting in frequent flight delays. The over-weight bag fee is designed to encourage passengers to pack multiple pieces of luggage instead of one large piece—even with more small bags, studies have shown that there is no appreciable delay in loading and unloading airplanes.

We hope that this change will result in fewer flight delays, increasing the reliability of Pacific Airways arrival and departure times, so you can be confident in making connections and arriving at your desired destinations when you expect.

---

162.   What is the main topic of this notice?

   (A) A change in baggage rates
   (B) A change of arrival and departure times
   (C) A change in a flight connection
   (D) A report on flight delays

163.   What did the cited study demonstrate?

   (A) Pacific Airways is slower than other companies at unloading bags
   (B) Pacific Airways is faster than other companies at unloading bags
   (C) Small bags delay flights
   (D) Large bags delay flights

164.   What is the purpose of the luggage fee increase?

   (A) To encourage people to use smaller bags
   (B) To encourage people to use larger bags
   (C) To encourage people to fly Pacific Airways
   (D) To slow down the loading and unloading of airplanes

Questions 165 through 168 refer to the following phone message.

WHILE YOU WERE OUT

TO Amanda Pratt   **DATE** 2/11/09   **TIME** 3:33 pm

FROM Isaac Zimmerman   **OF** United Tax Specialists

PHONE 1-800-533-2334 ext. 20   **FAX** 1-800-533-2347

_____ Came to See You	**REMARKS** Isaac called to apologize for not returning your call last week
✓ Telephoned	and to say that your 2008 federal tax forms are ready—he just needs to
_____ Will Call Again	know whether to send them by courier or if you will pick them up
✓ Please Phone	yourself. If you give him a call by 4:45 he can have a courier get them to
	us by 5:30 today.

SIGNED David Kline

---

165. What kind of office does Mr. Zimmerman probably work in?

(A) A tax accountancy office
(B) A courier dispatch office
(C) A telephone company office
(D) A federal government office

166. Why did Mr. Zimmerman call?

(A) To tell Ms. Pratt about some completed forms
(B) To tell Mr. Kline his tax forms are ready
(C) To apologize for sending some tax forms
(D) To have a courier deliver his tax forms

167. According to the message, what does Ms. Pratt need to do?

(A) Wait for Mr. Zimmerman to call
(B) Call a personal courier to deliver tax forms
(C) Send Mr. Zimmerman his 2008 tax forms
(D) Call Mr. Zimmerman

168. Why did Mr. Zimmerman apologize?

(A) Because he called Ms. Pratt too early
(B) For not calling Ms. Pratt earlier
(C) For leaving tax forms with a courier
(D) Because he does not have Ms. Pratt's tax forms completed

Questions 169 through 172 refer to the following fax.

Fax

Date: 1/2/2010
To: Reservation Agent, Linton Hotel
Fax: 904-234-2123

From: Raylene Urich
Fax: 341-987-0987
Subject: Reservation Confirmation
Pages: 1

I am just writing to confirm my room reservation, which I made over the phone earlier this week. To restate my reservation, I will be arriving on May 12th and leaving the morning of May 18th. I also asked for a non-smoking room with a Queen-sized bed, kitchenette, and ocean-view; from your website, it looks like this describes most of your rooms, so I hope these requests can be met. As I told the reservation agent I talked with, I will be arriving very early that morning (at 7:00 a.m.) and would like to leave my bags with you during the morning hours until check-in (which, if I remember, is 4:00 p.m.). In addition, because my flight leaves so late on May 18th, I would like to leave my bags at the front desk until 8:00 p.m. that day—is that okay?

Please send me a fax or email reconfirming my reservation and room requests. I look forward to your reply.

Sincerely,

Raylene Urich

---

169. What is the purpose of this fax?

(A) To confirm a reservation
(B) To make a reservation
(C) To respond to a reservation request
(D) To ask for the location of a hotel

170. What is Raylene NOT requesting?

(A) A room with a small kitchen
(B) A pet-friendly room
(C) A room with a view of the ocean
(D) A non-smoking room

171. At approximately what time will Raylene be arriving at Linton Hotel on May 12th?

(A) 7:00 a.m.
(B) 4:00 p.m.
(C) 7:00 p.m.
(D) 8:00 p.m.

172. How did Raylene first reserve her room?

(A) By fax
(B) By email
(C) By phone
(D) By the hotel's website

Questions 173 through 176 refer to the following memo.

Memo

To: All sales staff
From: Randal Smith, Head of Sales & Marketing
Re: Future sales meetings
Date: June 2nd

Last week I talked with our boss, and she agreed that something needs to be done about our monthly sales meetings. Because last month's sales meeting ran over its scheduled time by over an hour, Flora suggested we institute new procedures regarding meeting agendas. After consulting with the head of the Human Resources office, I've come up with what I believe are a number of changes to how we currently plan and run meetings. These changes will hopefully help us keep our meetings to their normal 2 hours. Please read the new policies below.

1.   Sales staff must write any topics they wish to discuss at the sales meeting on the agenda sheet posted in the main office before the day of the meeting. Only 3 topics can be added to the agenda sheet by any sales staff person. Two additional topic slots will be reserved for myself and Flora.

2.   Only topics already on the agenda can be discussed at monthly sales meetings.

3.   Discussion of any single agenda item will be limited to 20 minutes. Nancy has volunteered to keep track of the time. If a discussion hits 20 minutes, then it will be added to next month's agenda.

These changes will be in effect for our June meeting. If you have any questions regarding these changes, don't hesitate to contact me, but know that these changes will occur. Thank you for your cooperation.

---

173.   What is the main purpose of the memo?

(A) To inform staff of a policy change
(B) To set up a sales meeting
(C) To ask for suggestions on changing a
    policy
(D) To ask for submissions to next
    month's sales meeting agenda

174.   How long did last month's staff meeting
        most likely last?

(A) 1 hour
(B) Less than 2 hours
(C) 2 hours
(D) Over 3 hours

175.   Who is responsible for making sure
        discussions do not run too long?

(A) Flora
(B) Nancy
(C) Randal
(D) The Human Resources head manager

176.   What happens if a discussion runs longer
        than 20 minutes?

(A) It is continued via office email
(B) Mr. Smith decides if the discussion
    should continue
(C) It is added to the following meeting's
    agenda
(D) Mr. Smith sends out a memo

Questions 177 through 180 refer to the following advertisement.

Data and Electronic Service Librarian Assistant
Libraries and Information Services, Yorktown College Library

RESPONSIBILITIES
This position will work under the direction of the Director of the Social Science Libraries and Information Services (SSLIS). This position's responsibilities are:

- Develop, maintain and provide service for the library's Data Archive.
- Collaborate with the Social Science department on building college information databases.
- Develop and provide coordinated services to meet the full range of data needs at Yorktown in the Social Science department.
- Work with other Yorktown College staff and faculty to plan and implement a means of developing, maintaining and providing access to the Data Archive.

QUALIFICATIONS
    Required:
    1. Masters of Library Science or related field.
    2. Minimum of two years of relevant professional experience.
    3. Knowledge of various kinds of academic and/or government documents.
    4. Experience using library catalog software and internet-based information systems.
    5. Systematic approach to work, attention to detail, and ability to manage a broad variety of tasks and shifting priorities.
    6. Demonstrated ability to work effectively with others.

    Preferred:
    1. Experience in collection development, reference, and instruction in an academic or research library.

If you wish to apply for this position, please mail your resume along with a cover letter to Hermione Ploggins, Yorktown College Human Resources Dept., Campus Box 157, Yorktown, IL 84023, by April 1, 2009

---

177.   What type of advertisement is this?

        (A) A job ad for position in a human
            resources department
        (B) A job ad to fill the position of director of
            SSLIS
        (D) A job ad for a position in a social
            science department
        (D) A job ad for a librarian aide

178.   What is a duty of this position?

        (A) Earn a Masters of Library Services
        (B) Work with the computer science
            department
        (C) Maintain a website
        (D) Help improve library databases

179.   What is NOT a necessary skill for this job?

        (A) Two years of professional experience
            related to library studies
        (B) Attention to details
        (C) Knowledge on how to collect library
            materials
        (D) Knowledge on how to use library
            catalog software

180.   How does an applicant submit their
        resume?

        (A) Mail it to the human resources office
        (B) Attach it to an email
        (C) Send it by fax
        (D) Go to the human resources
            department

Questions 181 through 185 refer to the following emails.

From: polly.w@organics.ne.com
To: tim.r@organics.ne.com
CC: zack.t@ organics.ne.com
BCC: mary.n@ organics.ne.com
Re: Holiday Hours
Date: 12/1/09
Attachments: 09holidaywksch.doc

Hi Tim,

I just wanted to get back to you regarding your work schedule during the upcoming Christmas break. As we discussed, we will have reduced hours during the last two weeks of December, and will need someone to be in every weekday morning (save for Christmas Day, of course) to open the display store and help us get ready for the day. I talked with Zack about how to accommodate your request to have as much time off as possible, and to possibly let you take a day off on Christmas Eve. Zack said he could help open up on Christmas Eve; however, because you've used up your Personal Days for this year, you will need to take a "Sick Day" for Christmas Eve—Mary in Human Resources can help you with that, if you need to know how to record that information on your timesheet to make sure you get paid the correct amount.

Let's meet next week and go over the schedule for those weeks—I'll ask Zack to be at the meeting, too. Let me know if you have any questions.

Polly

From: tim.r@organics.ne.com
To: polly.w@organics.ne.com
CC: zack.t@ organics.ne.com
Re: Re: Holiday Hours
Date: 12/3/09

Hi Polly,

Thanks for sending me the break schedule. I've had a chance to look it over, and had a few concerns. First, the schedule states I have to be in at 7:00 every morning; however, on Sundays we normally don't open until 9:00, so do I really have to be in 2 hours before we open the doors? It usually takes less than an hour to get the store set up for customers, so can I come in at 8:00 every Sunday instead?

Another issue we need to address is keys—with all of the morning staff (save for myself, of course) on vacation, we need to make sure Zack has a key when he opens the store by himself on Dec. 24th. Can you make a key for him by the meeting you talked about? I'll make sure Zack knows all the procedures for the morning shift by the time Christmas Eve arrives.

Lastly, and most importantly, I saw that according to the schedule I only have two days off between Dec. 15th and Jan. 5th—this was not what I was hoping for in terms of a work schedule. When I originally agreed to do the bulk of the Christmas break openings, I was expecting to have at least three days off, not including Christmas. I would like to see if there is anyone who can do my shift for two more days. I would be happy to come in during my off time and show them how to open the display store.

Tim

181.   What is the main purpose for the email sent
        by Polly?

        (A) To tell Tim about the holiday-break work
            schedule
        (B) To ask Mary for help with a timesheet
        (C) To ask Tim for his Christmas break
            schedule
        (D) To ask Zack to attend a meeting

182.   What time does the display store open most
        days?

        (A) 5:00
        (B) 7:00
        (C) 8:00
        (D) 9:00

183.   Tim is concerned about all the following
        issues EXCEPT

        (A) Not having enough days off during the
            holiday break
        (B) Having to take a sick day for one of his
            days off
        (C) A coworker doesn't have the proper key
            to open the store
        (D) Having to come in earlier than normal on
            Sundays

184.   Which of the following is most likely true?

        (A) Tim does not want to work holidays
        (B) Tim does not normally work holidays
        (C) Zack does not normally work holidays
        (D) Zack does not normally open the store

185.   Excluding Christmas, how many days is Tim
        now hoping to have off during the holiday
        break?

        (A) 2
        (B) 3
        (C) 4
        (D) 5

Questions 186 through 190 refer to the following memo and schedule.

Memo
To: All moderators From: Tina Pomogrino, Room Coordinator Re: Room Schedule Change Date: 7/10/09 Attached to this memo you'll find the revised discussion room assignments for our PSE conference next week. As you can see, we fixed the room assignment issue raised during our teleconference yesterday—now, Carlos Montoya doesn't need to be in two rooms at once! You will note that because Pete Williams needs to leave at lunch due to a last-minute business meeting; we have given his afternoon discussion to Rachel Ross. Thanks, Rachel, for volunteering to take his spot on such short notice. Thank you once again for all your hard work and dedication in making our upcoming conference a success!

Pacific State Educators Conference Schedule - WEDNESDAY, JULY 15, 2009

Time				
10:00-12:00 pm	**Cypress Room** Moderator: Montoya **Tracking your Teaching**: How to Easily Maintain Student Assessments	**Spruce Room** Moderator: Ross **The Student Creator**: Hands-on Activities for Student Creation	**Willow Room** Moderator: Williams **Internet Ideas**: Online Educational Resources	**Birch Room** Moderator: Richards **Teacher Teamwork**: Supporting Struggling Faculty
12:00-1:00 pm	Lunch			
1:00-3:00 pm	**Cypress Room** Moderator: Holton **They Need You**: Integrating Special Needs Students into a Traditional Curriculum	**Douglas Room** Moderator: Ross **Manage It!**: Strategies for Effective Classroom Management	**Willow Room** Moderator: Carey **Dramatic Delivery**: Benefits of Learning Through Theatre	**Birch Room** Moderator: Wright **Teaching Cooperation**: The Role of Social Activities in Faculty Cohesion
3:15-5:15 pm	**Cypress Room** Moderator: Carey **Digital Dialogue**: Using Digital Media to Share Teaching Ideas	**Douglas Room** Moderator: Montoya **The Power of Opposites**: How to use Debate as a Teaching Tool	**Willow Room** Moderator: Ross **The Laboratory Classroom**: Transforming your Classroom into a Scientific Lab	**Birch Room** Moderator: Richards **Storytelling**: How narratives can aid in teaching
5:15-6:15 pm	**Diamond Room** Reception			

186.   What is the main purpose of the memo?

(A) To ask for suggestions on changing
     room assignments at a conference
(B) To set up a teleconference call
(C) To notify moderators of changes to a
     conference schedule
(D) To ask for volunteers to replace a
     moderator

187.   Who moderates the most?

(A) Montoya
(B) Richards
(C) Ross
(D) Carey

188.   What was probably wrong with the previous
        draft of the conference schedule?

(A) Montoya was assigned to moderate in
     different rooms at the same time
(B) Pete Williams didn't want to moderate
     any meetings
(C) Rachel Ross wanted to moderate more
     meetings
(D) There were not enough moderators for
     the conference

189.   According to the memo, why does Williams
        only moderate one discussion?

(A) He only wanted to moderate one
     meeting
(B) He needs to attend a meeting after lunch
     that day
(C) He is volunteering for another
     conference
(D) He wanted to give his afternoon
     discussion assignment to Ross

190.   Which pair of meetings would a participant
        NOT be able to attend?

(A) Both "Student Creator" and "Laboratory
     Classroom"
(B) Both "Teacher Teamwork" and
     "Storytelling"
(C) Both Teaching Cooperation" and
     "Manage It"
(D) Both "They Need You" and "Digital
     Dialogue"

Questions 191 through 195 refer to the following letter and invoice.

Customer Service Department
Regency Sound & Lighting Rental (RSL Rentals)
4526 SE Stark
Portland, OR 98344

October 2, 2008

REF: #1047
Sacred Hills Wedding Chapel
12344 SE Wanda Drive
Portland, OR 98354

Dear Mr. Iglesias,

I am writing in reference to an overdue payment for Invoice #1047. As you can see from the attached copy of the invoice, you still owe over half the total cost for renting our sound equipment on August 17th—in fact, the only payment we have received at this time was the security deposit which you made when you originally ordered our equipment. With previous rentals your company has always been timely in its payments to RSL Rentals, so when we did not receive payment at the end of August, we tried to contact you to remind you of your payment—however, we were only able to leave a message; since then, we have left two other messages but have never received a return call.

We regret to inform you that failure to pay your balance in full by October 15, 2008 will result in us taking you to small claims court where we will use all legal means to get payment. This will be our last communication regarding this matter. Please note that you can pay by either check or credit card.

We look forward to your prompt reply.

Sincerely,

Jon Weyr
Head Service Director

INVOICE

Regency Sound & Lighting Rentals
4526 SE Stark
Portland, OR 98344

Order Date: 8/10/08
Invoice #: 1047
P.O.#: N/A

Bill To:
Sacred Hills Wedding Chapel
ATTN: Bill Iglesias

Deliver To:
12344 SE Wanda Drive
Portland, OR 98354
513-123-4567

Delivery Date: 8/17/08
Due Date: 8/30/08

Description	Qty	Unit Cost	Amount
Boom Microphone (incl. cables & stands)	4	$35.00	$140.00
Speakers (incl. cables)	4	$45.00	$180.00
Sound Mixer with Amp	1	$150.00	$150.00
CD & MP3 Player (incl. cables)	1	$20.00	$20.00
		Subtotal	$490.00
		Sales Tax (4.5%)	$22.05
		Total	$512.05
		Payments/Credits	$250.00
		Balance Due	$262.05

191.   What is the purpose of the letter?

(A) To inform Mr. Iglesias of an overdue
        payment
(B) To pay an overdue bill
(C) To ask for more time to pay a bill
(D) To ask Mr. Iglesias to pay for an
        upcoming rental

192.   What kind of company does Jon Weyr
        probably work for?

(A) A church
(B) A equipment rental company
(C) A credit card company
(D) A wedding caterer

193.   Before this letter, how many times had the
        RSL Rentals tried to contact Mr. Iglesias?

(A) None
(B) 1
(C) 2
(D) 3

194.   By when does Mr. Iglesias need to pay RSL
        Rentals or else be taken to court?

(A) August 15
(B) August 17
(C) August 30
(D) October 15

195.   How much was the security deposit?

(A) $250
(B) $262.05
(C) $490.00
(D) $512.05

Questions 196 through 200 refer to the following letter and purchase order.

Date: 4/14/2008
To: Ms. Peters, Giovanni & Sons, CPA
Fax: 904-234-2123

From: Greg Barton, Richmond Office Supplies
Fax: 341-987-0987
Re: P.O.: #001345
Pages: 2

Dear Ms. Peters,

    Thank you for your recent order to our company. However, we need to change the method of payment you listed on the P.O.; I'm afraid that Richmond Office Supplies does not allow, for orders exceeding $50, the kind of payment you wish to make. Instead, you can pay by credit card, cash or money order. Alternately, checks are also acceptable, provided it is a business check, not a personal check. Please contact me as soon as possible to let us know how you wish to pay.

    In addition, you will remember that when we talked on the phone on 4/10/08 I told you about an additional $25 delivery fee which you would need to pay if you wish us to deliver your order to your office. This fee will need to be paid at the time you make payment for the rest of the order.

    I also need to inform you that we no longer carry pens in the color you ordered. If you would like to change your order, we have pens in black, blue or green.

    Lastly, we would need to discuss what days you are able to receive our delivery. Let me know if you can only accept deliveries during your normal weekday work hours (I understand those to be 8am-5pm, Mon-Fri), or if there will be someone at your office on the weekend—if so, then we could deliver your order on Saturday between 8am-12pm. If you are unable to accept deliveries during the weekend, then the earliest we can get your supplies to you would be Monday.

    I look forward to your response to this fax.

Sincerely,

Greg Barton
Customer Service

	Purchase Order			ORDER No: 001345	
				SHIP TO:	Giovanni & Sons, CPA 123 Yarborough Lane Richmond Hill, RI 45234
VENDOR:	Richmond Office Supplies 415 Main Street Richmond Hill, RI 45230			**BILL TO:**	Giovanni & Sons, CPA *(same as above)*

CUSTOMER ACCOUNT No:	CUSTOMER CONTACT:	DATE OF ORDER:
G-423	Rhonda Peters	4/12/08
PAYMENT:	**CUSTOMER TEL:**	**DESIRED DELIVERY DATE:**
C.O.D.	905-555-2345	ASAP

ITEM	STOCK NUMBER	QUANTITY	UNIT COST	TOTAL COST
Pencils, box #2, red	32145-12	5	2.50	12.50
Xerox Paper-case	78-354-23	12	30.00	360.00
Pens, box, red, fine point	89234-12	10	5.00	50.00
Tape, 1" case	543-980	3	12.50	37.50
Staples, box	5234-34	10	1.00	10.00
Letter-size envelopes	57-123-70	2	12.00	24.00
			NET TOTAL:	494.00

196.   What is not a purpose of the letter?

(A) To remind a customer about an
        additional fee
(B) To apologize for not filling an order
(C) To set up a delivery date
(D) To inform a customer about the methods
        for paying for an order

197.   Which method can Ms. Peters NOT use to
        pay for her order?

(A) Credit Card
(B) Cash on delivery
(C) Cash
(D) Business Check

198.   How much does it cost for Richmond Office
        Supplies to deliver an order?

(A) $25
(B) $50
(C) $494
(D) $519

199.   Which of the following is most likely true?

(A) Mr. Barton does not want to deliver the
        supplies to Ms. Peters
(B) Mr. Barton never told Ms. Peters about
        the delivery fee before his fax
(C) Ms. Peters forgot to add the delivery fee
        to the P.O.
(D) Ms. Peters didn't know about the
        delivery fee when writing the P.O.

200.   What does Richmond Office Supplies no
        longer keep in stock?

(A) Red paper
(B) Red pencils
(C) Red pens
(D) Blue pens

Answers to the Reading Comprehension Quiz are on Page 129

Reading Comprehension Answers

(Method, pages 101-109)   *(Quiz, pages 112-129)*

Questions 1-6 answered in Class Discussions

7.	B	153.	C	177. D
8.	D	154.	B	178. D
9.	C	155.	C	179. C
10.	B	156.	B	180. A
11.	D	157.	D	181. A
		158.	B	182. C
Questions 12-14 answers will vary		159.	C	183. B
		160.	D	184. D
		161.	A	185. C
		162.	A	186. C
		163.	D	187. C
		164.	A	188. A
		165.	A	189. B
		166.	A	190. C
		167.	D	191. A
		168.	B	192. B
		169.	A	193. D
		170.	B	194. D
		171.	A	195. A
		172.	C	196. B
		173.	A	197. B
		174.	D	198. A
		175.	B	199. C
		176.	C	200. C

Appendix A

TOEIC Tricks

Photograph Tricks

Extreme Inference. These wrong Answer Choices will give a statement for which there is no (or very little) information from the photograph to support the statement.

Answer: They are negotiating a deal.

Similar-sounding Word. These wrong Answer Choices will use words which sound similar to words seen in the photograph.

Answer: They are meeting around the cable.

Wrong Object. These wrong Answer Choices will refer to Nouns that are not seen in the Photograph, but will often be words associated with the other words in the Photograph.

Answer: The copier is on the table.

Wrong Action. These wrong Answer Choices will use Verbs not seen in the Photograph, but will often be words associated with the other words in the Photograph.

Answer: They are arriving at a meeting.

Wrong Relationship/Location. These wrong Answer Choices will use prepositions that create the wrong relationship between Nouns in the Photograph.

Answer: The screen is on the table.

Wrong Condition. These wrong Answer Choices will use adjectives that give wrong descriptions of the Nouns in the Photographs.

Answer: The screen is broken.

Question-Response Tricks

> **Question**: *Can you drive the boss to tomorrow's meeting?*

Similar-Sounding Words. Listen for near-homophones (Ex: "freeze" and "sneeze"). If the word sounds strange, it might be the wrong word!

Answer: I don't know when the bus leaves.

Topic-Related Words. These wrong Responses use words related to the topic of the Question, but give information that the Question does not ask for.

Answer: We need to discuss the sales report.

Word Repetition. Like other sections of the TOEIC, many wrong Responses will repeat words or phrases from the Question but not be correct answers. In English, important words from Questions are *usually* not repeated in Answers to Questions. Also, beware of words that can be **both nouns and verbs** (Ex: "*can*").

Answer: The meeting was very informative.

Wrong Question Type. These wrong Responses will use pieces of information from the Question, but they are answers to a different type of Question.

Answer: It's at the branch office.

Wrong Subject/Object. These wrong Responses will use the correct Question Type ("*where*"), but refer to different Subject or Object ("*someone*" Question and a "*something*" Response) than the Question.

Answer: She would be happy to.

Wrong Verb Tense. These wrong Responses will use an incorrect verb tense. For example, the Question is asking about the future, but the Response uses the past tense.

Answer: Yes, I drove him to the meeting.

Short Conversations Tricks

Man: *Can you help me with this report? I'm having a hard time formatting it.*

Woman: *Well, I don't know much about that program you're using, but Robert might be more help. He's great at making documents look their best. He knows how to fix reports up quick.*

Man: *Thanks! I'll give him a call right now. My deadline for it is tomorrow's meeting.*

Woman: *Oh no, that reminds me—I need to print my report for a meeting in an hour!*

Extreme Inference. These wrong Answer Choices will give a conclusion that is possible, but there is no (or very little) information from the conversation to support the conclusion.

> *Question*: What will the man do next?"
> *Answer*: Ask his boss for an extension.

Incorrect Paraphrase. Wrong Answer Choices will often use words and ideas from the conversation but change them slightly. They may use the wrong idiom ("*take over*" vs. "*take out*"), or they may add an extreme word (ex: "never" or "always") that makes the Answer Choice wrong.

> *Question*: Why can't the woman help the man?"
> *Answer*: She doesn't like working with a particular program.

Similar-Sounding Words. Listen for near-homophones ("please", "sneeze"). If the word sounds strange, it might be the wrong word!

> *Question*: What is Robert good at doing?"
> *Answer*: He's good at taking a rest.

Similar Tone. These wrong Answer Choices use words with a **similar positive/negative tone** as words and voices in the conversation, but use those words incorrectly.

> *Question*: How does the woman feel about helping the man?"
> *Answer*: She is sorry to help him.

Topic-Related. These wrong Answer Choices use words related to the topic of the conversation, but talk about information that the conversation does not say. Students are often tricked by these kinds of Answer Choices because they use their personal knowledge, not information from the conversation.

> *Question*: What will *the man* do next?"
> *Answer*: Go on a coffee break.

Wrong Action. Some answer choices look correct because they use many words you heard from the conversation, but describe the wrong action.

> *Question*: Why is the man asking for help?"
> *Answer*: It's too hard to fix a program.

Wrong Person. Many wrong Answer Choices will be pieces of information you heard from the conversation, but will be wrong because the other speaker said the information.

> *Question*: What will *the man* do next?"
> *Answer*: *He* will print a report.

Short Talks Tricks

> **Woman**: *Good afternoon, ladies and gentlemen. I would like to introduce you to the keynote speaker of this year's sales conference. Daniel Oliveri has been a leading voice in the field of online-marketing over the last four years, developing many innovative strategies which have become industry standards. Before this, Mr. Oliveri spent a decade in the field of webpage design, working for Apple Computers, building websites that were user-friendly, rich in content, artistically designed, and providing companies with information to help them better serve their customers. Tonight he will be speaking on the theme of this conference: how to create a 5-step plan to draw potential customers to your website through online advertising. Everyone, please join me in welcoming Daniel Oliveri.*

Extreme Inference. These wrong Answer Choices will give a conclusion that is possible, but there is no (or very little) information from the conversation to support the conclusion.

Question: How long did Mr. Oliveri design web pages?"
Answer: 14 years.

Incorrect Paraphrase. Wrong answers will often use words and ideas from the talk but change them slightly, making them incorrect. Often they will add words such as "never" or "always".

Question: What will Mr. Oliveri talk about?"
Answer: How to become an online customer.

Similar Types of Detail. When dates, times or locations are given, listen for similar types of information. In the Short Talks, there are usually three pieces of information of the same type, such as three different times of day, designed to confuse you.

Question: How long did Mr. Oliveri design web pages?"
Answer: Four years

Topic-Related. These wrong Answer Choices will be actions or reasons that possibly fit the *topic or situation* of the Talk, but not the *information* given in the Talk. For example, the Talk could be a phone call about "changing a hotel reservation", but the Answer Choice would be "make a complaint"—both of those actions (changing a reservation, complaining) are common reasons for people to make phone calls.

Question: What did Mr. Oliveri do for the last four years?"
Answer: Speak at sales conferences.

Word Repetition. These wrong Answer Choices will repeat words or phrases from the talk but will not be correct answers. Listen carefully to the nouns that numbers are connected to (*example*: "23 people" vs. "23 days").

Question: How many years has he been working in online marketing?"
Answer: Five years

Wrong Detail. These wrong Answer Choices will give *true information* that *was* heard in the Short Talk, but the information is *not* answering the actual Question.

Question: What did Mr. Oliveri create at Apple?"
Answer: *A 5-step plan for online ads*

Incomplete Sentence Tricks

> **Question**: Everyone is happy they will receive a 5% _____ under the new contract.

Limited Fit. These wrong Answer Choices use words that could fit if only the word before or after it was read, but *don't* fit the whole sentence.

Answer: down

Opposite Meaning. These wrong Answer Choices use words that are opposite in meaning to the correct answer, but usually *do* fit the sentence grammatically.

Answer: cut

Similar-Looking Words. These wrong Answer Choices use words that look similar to the correct answer, but because they have a different root word, their meanings are different.

Answer: praise

Similar Meaning. These wrong Answer Choices use words that have a similar meaning to the correct answer, but do not fit with the sentence grammatically or don't fit the Context of the sentence.

Answer: elevation

Topic-Related. These wrong Answer Choices use words related to the topic of the sentence but are not appropriate to the Situation of the Sentence, and often do not fit the sentence grammatically.

Answer: employment

Wrong Form. These wrong Answer Choices use the correct root word, but the ending of the word is wrong, turning it into a different Type of Word or the wrong Verb Tense. These wrong Answer Choices may also use the wrong preposition.

Answer: raising

Text Completion Tricks

> **Question**: The deadline for _____ for the in-house 'Innovations in Marketing' contest has been pushed back to March 22nd.

Opposite Meaning. These wrong Answer Choices use words that are opposite in meaning to the correct answer, but *may* fit the sentence grammatically.

Answer: withdrawals

Similar-Looking Word. These wrong Answer Choices use words that look similar to the correct answer, but because they have a different root word, their meanings are different.

Answer: subjecting

Similar Meaning. These wrong Answer Choices use words that have a similar meaning to the correct answer, but do not fit with the sentence grammatically, often due to **prepositions in the sentence** or the **subject of the sentence**.

Answer: applications

Topic-Related. These wrong Answer Choices use words related to the topic of the sentence but are not appropriate to the Situation of the Sentence, and often do not fit the sentence grammatically.

Answer: marketers

Wrong Form. These wrong Answer Choices use the correct root word but the wrong form of that word, making the Answer Choice not fit the sentence grammatically.

Answer: submits

Reading Comprehension Tricks

To: All sales staff
From: Randal Smith, Head of Sales & Marketing
Re: Future sales meeting
Date: June 2nd

Because last month's sales meeting ran over its scheduled time by over an hour, we will be instituting new procedures regarding meeting agendas. These changes will hopefully help us keep our meetings to their normal 2 hours. Please read the new procedures below.

1.   Sales staff must write any topics they wish to discuss at the sales meeting on the agenda sheet posted in the main office before the day of the meeting. Only 3 topics can be added to the agenda sheet by any sales staff person. Two additional topic slots will be reserved for myself.

2.   Only topics already on the agenda can be discussed at monthly sales meetings.

These changes will take effect for our June meeting. If you have any questions regarding these changes, don't hesitate to contact me, but know that these changes will occur. Thank you for your cooperation.

Incorrect Paraphrase. These wrong Answer Choices will often use words and ideas from the Text but change them slightly, making them incorrect.

Question: How can someone add a topic to June's meeting agenda?"
Answer: Add to agenda email

Similar Type of Information. When dates, times or locations are given, look for similar types of information—there are usually three pieces of information of the same type.

Question: How many topics can be added by any sales staff person?"
Answer: 2

Topic-Related. These wrong Answer Choices use words related to the topic of the Text, but give information that the Text does not provide. Students are often tricked by these kinds of Answer Choices because they use their personal knowledge, not information from the Text.

"NOT" Questions usually use this Trick to hide correct answers.

Question: What is not a new procedure for sales meetings?"
Answer: Ask Mr. Smith to add topic.

Word Repetition. Like other sections of the TOEIC, many wrong Answer Choices will repeat words or phrases from the Text but not be correct answers.

Question: How long did May's sales meeting last?"
Answer: An hour.

Wrong Detail. These wrong Answers will use true details from the Text to answer Questions related to a different piece of information; thus, making them incorrect answers for that specific question.

Question: How can someone add a topic to June's meeting agenda?"
Answer: Contact Mr. Smith.

Extreme Inference. Many wrong answers will use strong Adverbs ("never", "always", "too"), Helping Verbs ("must", "cannot", "need to") or very strong Adjectives ("happy", "broken", "tall")—you should think of these kinds of words as **"Extreme Words"**. Extreme Words will often make Answer Choices wrong, even though every other word in the Answer Choice could be correct.

When you see any Extreme Word in an Answer Choice, look carefully for it (or its synonym) in the Text.

Question: Why are the changes taking place?
Answer: Mr. Smith was angry at the length of the last meeting.

Appendix B

Types of Texts

In Part 7 (and Part 6) of the TOEIC, students will see various kinds of Texts. Students will need to be able to quickly and easily find the Headings and Titles for each kind. Students will also want to know where the Topic and Purpose of the Text is most likely located.

On the following pages are different types of Texts you may see on the TOEIC. Study these pages and the information inside the white boxes given about each type of Text.

Advertisement

Advertisements (also called "ads") can often look like other types of Texts—sometimes they look like Letters (**page 140**) or Notices (**page 143**). However, they will all have certain pieces of information:

Are you paying too much calling overseas?

> **The Teaser**: The Title of an Ad is often called a "teaser", hinting at what they are selling, but NOT TELLING YOU DIRECTLY.

Do you feel that with the money you spent calling a friend or loved one in another country you could have flown to see them?

> The first 1-2 sentences of an Ad often do not give the MAIN IDEA or PURPOSE of the Ad, but hint at it.

Don't let that h

Save 50% on your next international phone call when you switch to CONNEXUS, the leading international telecommunication company in over 30 countries. Simply call 1-800-CONNEXUS, and tell us which country you call the most—and lock in a 50% discount for all calls to that country for the next year! We will even help you in switching from your current international call carrier to us by contacting your current carrier and doing all the work join CONNEXUS!

> **The Call to Action**: This is the MAIN IDEA of the Ad, telling the reader what they SHOULD DO.

We understand that with family and friends all over the world, you need an inexpensive and reliable service to help you keep in touch with those you love--CONNEXUS, with over 10 years experience and one of the most advanced networks on the planet, is there for you.

> **Why Us?**: This is the part of the Ad explains WHY you SHOULD USE the product or company.

Email

Emails can take different forms and styles, but the structure is usually the same as seen on this page.

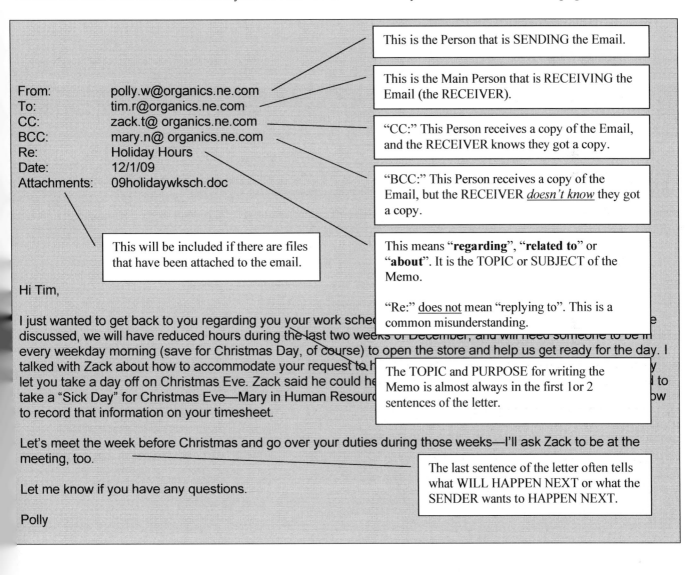

Fax

Faxes can take different forms and styles, so the structure you see on this page may not be exactly what you see on Test Day—some pieces of information may not be included in every Fax, or the information will be in a different order; however, most of the same types of information will be given.

Sometimes a Fax will look like a Letter *(see **Page 140**)*, but will have Fax Numbers instead of Addresses.

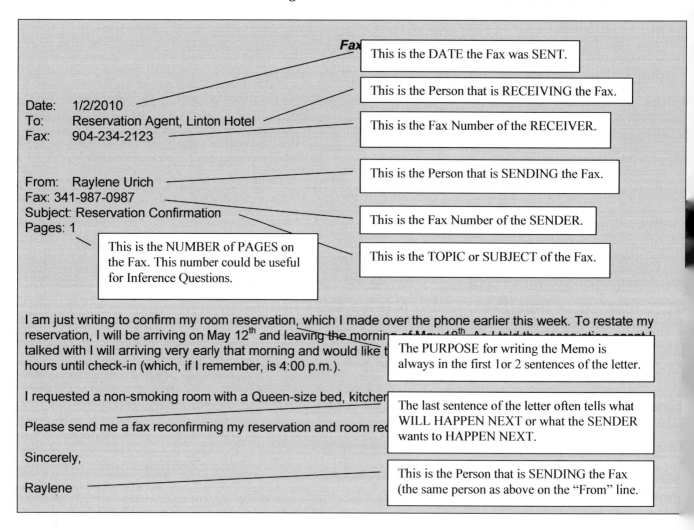

Fax

This is the DATE the Fax was SENT.

This is the Person that is RECEIVING the Fax.

This is the Fax Number of the RECEIVER.

This is the Person that is SENDING the Fax.

This is the Fax Number of the SENDER.

This is the TOPIC or SUBJECT of the Fax.

Date: 1/2/2010
To: Reservation Agent, Linton Hotel
Fax: 904-234-2123

From: Raylene Urich
Fax: 341-987-0987
Subject: Reservation Confirmation
Pages: 1

This is the NUMBER of PAGES on the Fax. This number could be useful for Inference Questions.

I am just writing to confirm my room reservation, which I made over the phone earlier this week. To restate my reservation, I will be arriving on May 12th and leaving the morning of May 18th. As I told the reservation agent I talked with I will arriving very early that morning and would like t hours until check-in (which, if I remember, is 4:00 p.m.).

The PURPOSE for writing the Memo is always in the first 1 or 2 sentences of the letter.

I requested a non-smoking room with a Queen-size bed, kitchen

Please send me a fax reconfirming my reservation and room req

The last sentence of the letter often tells what WILL HAPPEN NEXT or what the SENDER wants to HAPPEN NEXT.

Sincerely,

Raylene

This is the Person that is SENDING the Fax (the same person as above on the "From" line.

Invoice

An Invoice is a form that REQUESTS PAYMENT for goods or services. It is sent by companies to people who owe them money, and includes a lists of items that person had purchased.

You will also want to study the Headings found on Purchase Orders (see *Page 145*)—sometimes Invoices use the same words in their Headings.

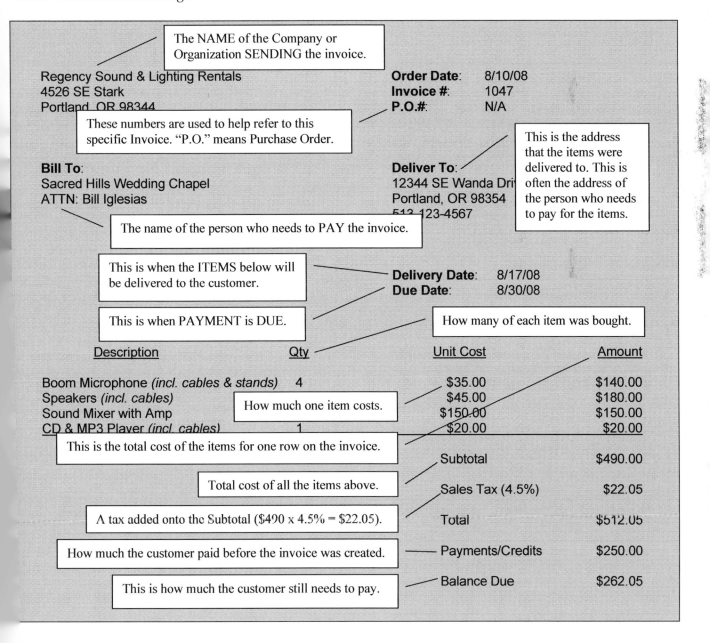

Job Advertisement

This type of Text is announcing a job available at a company. It is sometimes titled "Classified Ad", "Want Ad", "Job Ad", "Seeking Applicants" or "Open Position". It will usually include these pieces of information:

Position Offered

Data and Electronic Service Librarian ———————————————— | The TITLE of the position. |
Libraries and Information Services, Yorktown College Library

| The NAME of the Company or Organization looking to hire someone. |

RESPONSIBILITIES
Yorktown College is looking to fill the position of Data and Electronic Service Librarian, a position which will work under the direction of the Director of the Social Science Libraries and Information Services (SSLIS). This position has responsibility for:

| A brief description of what someone will DO in the position. |

- Develop, maintain and provide service
- Collaborate with various academic departments on building college information databases.
- Develop and provide coordinated services to meet the full range of data needs at Yorktown in the social science departments and in related programs and professional schools.
- Work with other Yorktown College staff and faculty to plan and implement a means of developing, maintaining and providing access to the Data Archive.

QUALIFICATIONS ————————————————

| A list of REQUIRED QUALIFICATIONS someone must have in order to be considered for the job. |

    Required:
    1. Masters of Library Science.
    2. Minimum of two years of relevant professional experience
    3. Subject knowledge of the various kinds of academ

| A list of PREFERRED QUALIFICATIONS ("skills") it is best for someone to have for the job. |

    4. Experience using library catalog software and inte
    5. Systematic approach to work, attention to detail, and ability to manage a broad variety of tasks and shifting priorities.
    6. Demonstrated ability to work effectively with others.

    Preferred:
    1. Experience in collection development, reference, and instruct

| This tells how to APPLY for the job. |

If you wish to apply for this position, please send your resume along with a coverletter to Hermione Ploggins, Yorktown College Human Resources Dept., Campus Box 157, Yorktown, IL 84023, by April 1, 2009

You *might* also see the following information:

- **CONTACT INFORMATION** (for example, "phone number" or "email") of someone that can answer questions about the job

- A list of **PREFERRED QUALIFICATIONS** ("skills") which are good (but not necessary) for someone to have for the job

Letter

Letters are a very common type of Text on the TOEIC. Letters are used for many different purposes, but most often they are used to INFORM CUSTOMERS or OTHER COMPANIES of something, or ASK someone for INFORMATION, HELP or SERVICE.

The location of certain important pieces of information will help in answering many Questions.

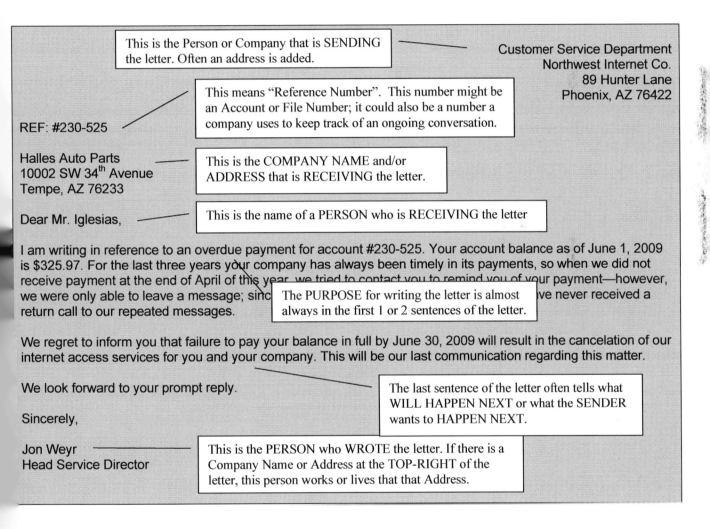

Memo

Memos (like some Announcements & Notices) are used to GIVE INFORMATION to an employee, a group of employees, or all employees. Memos look like E-mails.

When used to give information to employees, Notices *(see **Page 143**)* sometimes look like Memos.

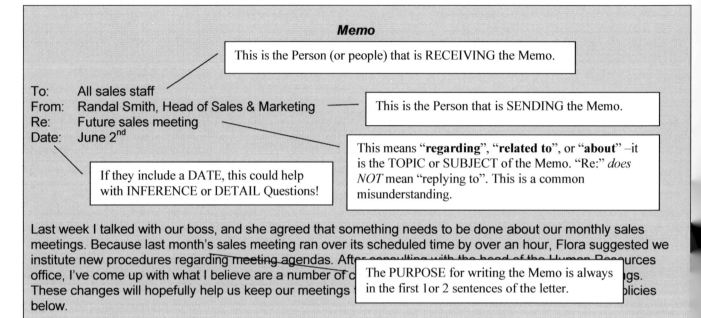

Memo

This is the Person (or people) that is RECEIVING the Memo.

To: All sales staff
From: Randal Smith, Head of Sales & Marketing
Re: Future sales meeting
Date: June 2nd

This is the Person that is SENDING the Memo.

If they include a DATE, this could help with INFERENCE or DETAIL Questions!

This means "**regarding**", "**related to**", or "**about**" –it is the TOPIC or SUBJECT of the Memo. "Re:" *does NOT* mean "replying to". This is a common misunderstanding.

Last week I talked with our boss, and she agreed that something needs to be done about our monthly sales meetings. Because last month's sales meeting ran over its scheduled time by over an hour, Flora suggested we institute new procedures regarding meeting agendas. After consulting with the head of the Human Resources office, I've come up with what I believe are a number of c[...]gs. These changes will hopefully help us keep our meetings [...]olicies below.

The PURPOSE for writing the Memo is always in the first 1or 2 sentences of the letter.

1. Sales staff must write any topics they wish to discuss at the sales meeting on the agenda sheet posted in the main office before the day of the meeting. Only 3 topics can be added to the agenda sheet by any sales staff person. Two additional topic slots will be reserved for myself and Flora.

2. Only topics already on the agenda can be discussed at monthly sales meetings.

3. Discussion of any single agenda item will be limited to 20 minutes. Nancy has volunteered to keep track of the time. If a discussion hits 20 minutes, then it will be added to next month's agenda.

These changes will take effect for our June meeting. If you have any questions regarding these changes, don't hesitate to contact me, but know that these changes will occur. Thank you for your cooperation.

Newspaper Article or News Report (+ News Release)

A News Article (sometimes called a "Report") is an article written for a newspaper or news website. The most important information (the "MAIN IDEA" or "MAIN TOPIC") is always given at the very beginning. As you move through the Article, information will become less and less important to the MAIN IDEA or MAIN TOPIC of the article—however, the TOEIC will probably still ask questions about these less important pieces of the Article.

A **News Release** looks very similar to a News Article. The difference is that a News Release is an <u>Announcement by a Company or Organization</u> GIVEN TO a news reporter so the that the information in News Release can be told to the public.

In some News Releases, the name of the PERSON SENDING the information and PERSON RECEIVING it are not included.

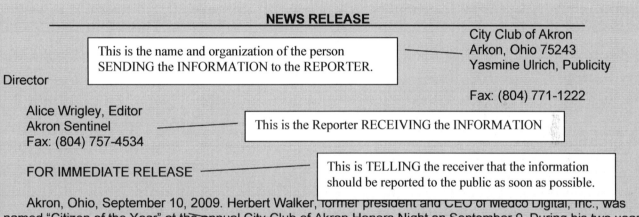

NEWS RELEASE

This is the name and organization of the person SENDING the INFORMATION to the REPORTER.

City Club of Akron
Arkon, Ohio 75243
Yasmine Ulrich, Publicity

Director

Fax: (804) 771-1222

Alice Wrigley, Editor
Akron Sentinel
Fax: (804) 757-4534

This is the Reporter RECEIVING the INFORMATION

FOR IMMEDIATE RELEASE

This is TELLING the receiver that the information should be reported to the public as soon as possible.

Akron, Ohio, September 10, 2009. Herbert Walker, former president and CEO of Medco Digital, Inc., was named "Citizen of the Year" at the annual City Club of Akron Honors Night on September 9. During his two years since leaving Medco Digital, Mr. Walker has been involved in dozens of philanthropic endeavors throughout the region, with a majority of those activities centered in Akron itself.

This first sentence gives the most important piece of information of the news release.

In accepting the award, Mr. Walker announced the kick off of [AEON?] [...] mic Opportunities Movement (AEON), dedicated to reducing the num[...] drive for donations, Mr. Walker promised that he would match every individual donation of $500, declaring that, "It is up to us, the fortunate members of the Akron community, to help lift up those among us less fortunate."

At the awards ceremony, Mr. Walker, aged 67, stated his never-ending desire to work on behalf of others, mainly due to his desire to help other achieve economic security and prosperity. He explained that, "My hometown has given me so much over the years," and that he has been "blessed with opportunities and aid which have help [me] achieve many things in business."

A native of Akron, Mr. Walker has been a longtime supporter of many local charities and non-profit organizations, helping out through personal donations, volunteering and fundraising campaigns. The list of his humanitarian activities was so long that according to Philip Regence, Akron City Club President, "It would have taken over 10 minutes to list all the things Herbert has done for our city and the state."

Notice

Notices (like Announcements) can be used to GIVE INFORMATION to employees, customers, or to all people in a certain location *(Example: airports, shopping malls, website)*. The people who are supposed to read the Notice are called the "Audience".

When used to give information to employees, Notices sometimes look like Memos *(see **Page 141**)*.

Notice to Passengers

This title *may* give a clue as to the AUDIENCE of the Notice.

Pacific Airways would like to inform passengers of a change in our baggage check-in policy—this policy takes effect March 1, 2010.

The PURPOSE for writing the Notice is always in the first sentence.

As of March 1, 2010, for bags weighing more than 40 lb[...] the normal $20 check-in luggage fee.

This change in check-in policy is to aid Pacific Airways in speed-up the loading and unloading of baggage onto airplanes. Studies conducted by several independent system analysis companies have found that large, heavy bags slow down the loading and unloading of airplanes resulting in frequent flight delays. The over weight bag fee is designed to encourage passengers to pack mult[...] bags, studies have shown that there is no appreciable [...]

More EXPLANATION for why the Information is being given is often found in the middle or end of the Notice.

We hope that this change will result in fewer flight delays, increasing the reliability of Pacific Airways arrival and departure times, so you can be confident in making connections and arriving at your desired destinations when you expect.

A DESIRED RESULT or GOAL is often found at the end of the Notice.

Phone Message

A Phone Message (sometimes just called a "Message") is a kind of short note used in the office to tell you if someone tried to talk to you *but you were busy or gone*.

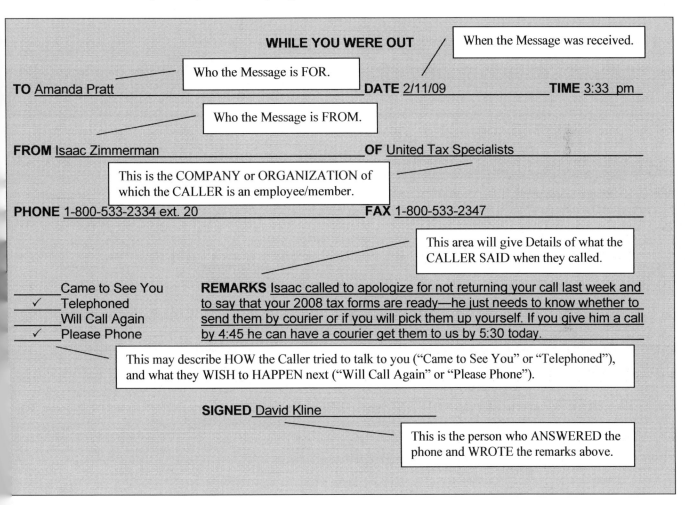

WHILE YOU WERE OUT

When the Message was received.

Who the Message is FOR.

TO Amanda Pratt   **DATE** 2/11/09   **TIME** 3:33 pm

Who the Message is FROM.

FROM Isaac Zimmerman   **OF** United Tax Specialists

This is the COMPANY or ORGANIZATION of which the CALLER is an employee/member.

PHONE 1-800-533-2334 ext. 20   **FAX** 1-800-533-2347

This area will give Details of what the CALLER SAID when they called.

_____ Came to See You	**REMARKS** Isaac called to apologize for not returning your call last week and
✓ Telephoned	to say that your 2008 tax forms are ready—he just needs to know whether to
_____ Will Call Again	send them by courier or if you will pick them up yourself. If you give him a call
✓ Please Phone	by 4:45 he can have a courier get them to us by 5:30 today.

This may describe HOW the Caller tried to talk to you ("Came to See You" or "Telephoned"), and what they WISH to HAPPEN next ("Will Call Again" or "Please Phone").

SIGNED David Kline

This is the person who ANSWERED the phone and WROTE the remarks above.

Purchase Order

A Purchase Order (also called a "P.O") is a form used to REQUEST goods or services. This is very similar to an Invoice (see **Page 138**). The *structure* of one Purchase Order can be very different from another Purchase Order, but they will almost all show certain pieces of information:

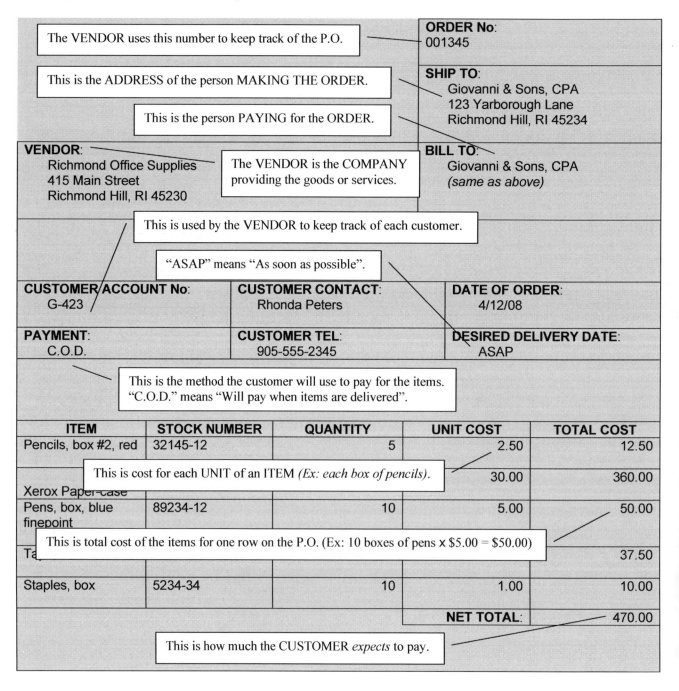

The VENDOR uses this number to keep track of the P.O.

ORDER No:
001345

This is the ADDRESS of the person MAKING THE ORDER.

This is the person PAYING for the ORDER.

SHIP TO:
Giovanni & Sons, CPA
123 Yarborough Lane
Richmond Hill, RI 45234

VENDOR:
Richmond Office Supplies
415 Main Street
Richmond Hill, RI 45230

The VENDOR is the COMPANY providing the goods or services.

BILL TO:
Giovanni & Sons, CPA
(same as above)

This is used by the VENDOR to keep track of each customer.

"ASAP" means "As soon as possible".

CUSTOMER ACCOUNT No:	CUSTOMER CONTACT:	DATE OF ORDER:
G-423	Rhonda Peters	4/12/08
PAYMENT: C.O.D.	**CUSTOMER TEL**: 905-555-2345	**DESIRED DELIVERY DATE**: ASAP

This is the method the customer will use to pay for the items. "C.O.D." means "Will pay when items are delivered".

ITEM	STOCK NUMBER	QUANTITY	UNIT COST	TOTAL COST
Pencils, box #2, red	32145-12	5	2.50	12.50
Xerox Paper, case			30.00	360.00
Pens, box, blue finepoint	89234-12	10	5.00	50.00
Ta...				37.50
Staples, box	5234-34	10	1.00	10.00
			NET TOTAL:	470.00

This is cost for each UNIT of an ITEM *(Ex: each box of pencils).*

This is total cost of the items for one row on the P.O. (Ex: 10 boxes of pens x $5.00 = $50.00)

This is how much the CUSTOMER *expects* to pay.

Schedule

A schedule will be a table which lists events—usually giving the <u>Time & Place</u> they occur, and often also telling the <u>Topic of the Event</u> and <u>Who is in Charge</u> of the event. It can be organized in several different ways (below is the most common style).

Conferences meetings and Seminars are often the kind of events given in a Schedule. Other common schedules are a Transportation Schedule (bus, train, or plane) or Trip Schedule (listing either Multiple Flights to different cities, or Multiple Locations in a single city where different events are being held.

Sometimes a Schedule will be included with a letter or memo, explaining what the Schedule is for—if you don't see a TITLE at the Schedule, then look for an explanation in the letter or memo.

Pacific State Educators Conference Schedule - WEDNESDAY, JULY 15, 2009

10:00-12:00 pm	Cypress Room Moderator: Coniglio Tracking your Teaching: How to Easily Maintain Student Assessments	Spruce Room Moderator: Ross The Student Crea... Activ... Creation	W... M... Internet Ideas: ...al	...ards Teacher Teamwork: Supporting Struggling Faculty
12:00-1:00 pm	**Diamond Room – Lunch**			
1:00-3:00 pm	Cypress Room Moderator: Holton They Need You: Integrating Special Needs Students into a Traditional Curriculum	Douglas Room Moderator: Ross Ma... Str... Effective Classroom Management	Willow Room Moderator: Carey ...very: ...arning Through Theatre	Birch Room Moderator: Wright Teaching Cooperation: The Role of Social Activities in Faculty Cohesion
3:15-5:15 pm	Cypress Room Moderator: Carey Digital Dialogue: Using Digital Media to Share Teaching Ideas	Douglas Room Moderator:... The Power of Opposites: How to use Debate as a Teaching Tool	Willow Room The Laboratory Classroom: Transforming your Classroom into a Scientific Lab	Birch Room ...r: Richards ...orytelling: How narratives can aid in teaching
5:15-6:15 pm	**Diamond Room – Reception**			

Callout annotations:
- This Title will tell you what EVENT or TRIP the Schedule is for.
- This Title will tell you WHERE an EVENT is taking place.
- "Moderator" is the PERSON in charge of a discussion or debate.
- Look for both TITLES and DESCRIPTIONS of the different events on a Schedule.

Table

Tables come in many styles. All Tables, though, will have Columns and Rows, and will often have Explanations or Additional Information above or below the table.

The Additional Information may give information about **exceptions** to the information in the table, so before answering Questions, make sure you skim above and below the Table to know what kind of information is there.

Shipping Rates for Walden Books

The Title will tell you what KIND OF INFORMATION is being given in the Table.

Domestic Standard*		Domestic Expedited#	Two Day	Overnight	International Standard*	International Expedited#
Books	$3.99	$6.99	$11.98	$17.98	$12.49	$35.98
CDs, Cassettes	$2.98	$5.19	$7.98	$11.98	$6.89	$32.98
VHS Videotapes	$2.98	$5.19	$11.98	$17.98	$12.29	$35.98
DVDs	$2.98	$5.19	$7.98	$11.98	$12.29	$32.98

*Standard: Domestic (U.S. & Canada): 9-12 Business Days / International: 13-18 Business days
 # Expedited: Domestic: 3-5 Business Days / International 6-8 Business days

This is an Explanation of CODES used in the Table, which will often be needed to answer certain Questions.

NOTE: All prices above are for packages weighing less than 20 lbs. For packages weighing 20 lbs. or more, all shipping rates are doubled.

This is Additional Information, which will often be needed to answer certain Questions.

Acknowledgements

I cannot adequately express my thanks to all the people who have helped me to create this book. Students, colleagues, friends and loved ones have all helped inspire me to write this book, and continue to motivate me to write and share all I have learned on how to Master English tests.

However, first and most important of those thanks goes to my wife, Julie Quinn, who has put up with my many hours typing on the computer. She has always been there to help me when I thought this book would never get done. This book is as much monument to her support as it is to my love of teaching English.

About this book

This book, *Master the TOEIC: Strategies – Teacher's Manual,* tries to use the simplest English possible to teach you the strategies for the TOEIC. I have tried to write this book for someone who may not understand complicated English.

If there is anything in this handbook that is confusing or difficult to understand, please contact me, Chris Quinn, at <u>chris@masterthetoeic.com</u> with your questions.

My goal is to give you the **best test preparation** possible!

12377234R00084

Printed in Great Britain
by Amazon.co.uk, Ltd.,
Marston Gate.